WOOD AS AN ENERGY RESOURCE

ACADEMIC PRESS RAPID MANUSCRIPT REPRODUCTION

WOOD AS AN ENERGY RESOURCE

David A. Tillman

Energy Correspondent
Area Development
Halcyon Business Publications, Inc.

1978
ACADEMIC PRESS   *New York   San Francisco   London*
A Subsidiary of Harcourt Brace Jovanovich, Publishers

ACADEMIC PRESS, INC.
111 Fifth Avenue, New York, New York 10003

United Kingdom Edition published by
ACADEMIC PRESS, INC. (LONDON) LTD.
24/28 Oval Road, London NW1 7DX

Tillman, David A.
    Wood as an energy resource

    Includes index.
    1. Wood as fuel. I. Title
TP324.T54   333.7'5   78-8252
ISBN 0-12-691260-2

PRINTED IN THE UNITED STATES OF AMERICA

FOR MILLIE

CONTENTS

PREFACE

The events precipitating our current reappraisal of fuels availability include the recognition that the world's resources of oil and natural gas, when pitted against demands for those clean and convenient fuels, are inadequate. Before the end of this century, resources of those fuels will be woefully inadequate. Compounding this problem is the acknowledgment that uranium, the hoped-for fuel of the future, is equally limited in availability. The most recent findings of the National Academy of Sciences paint a particularly bleak portrait of uranium resources and reserves for the coming decades. Given those stark situations, one must ask the question: With what policy should we address future energy supply issues?

The energy supply options include whether to put all of our eggs in a few baskets and watch those baskets intently, to paraphrase Mark Twain, or whether to put the energy eggs in many baskets, to paraphrase the earlier secular proverb. Rephrased, the question reads: Should the economy be electrified to the maximum degree and be fueled by breeder-based nuclear power and coal, or should the economy seek as many diverse sources of energy as possible? If the "few fuels" alternative becomes (or, some would say, remains) policy, then we must be prepared to accept a degree of fuel production centralization and a scale or activity unprecedented in history. If the "many fuels" approach is taken, we must be prepared to evaluate each energy source on the basis of how its contribution can best be made to the economy.

The policy question so stated includes but extends beyond technical and economic boundaries; it involves issues of national security, environmental quality, and above all overall philosophy. It is a question of whether to reject or accept solutions that may be applicable to only one region, area, or industry. It is a question of whether the national solution will dictate economic or geographic sector solutions, or whether economic entities will make individual contributions to the total solution.

The question is not whether to use coal and nuclear power. Coal will assume increasing importance for many years to come; and nuclear power will play an expanding role, limited by resource constraints and possibly the sociopolitical undesirability of breeder reactors. One of the key issues, therefore, is the extent to which alternatives can be employed to lessen the pressures now facing coal and other fuels. To what extent are such alternative fuels as wood desirable?

When evaluating one fuel it is a frequent practice to assert that such a fuel can supply, if not all, certainly a large percentage of U.S. energy needs. This practice is perpetrated regardless of whether the energy source under examination happens to be solar power, nuclear power, coal, or cattle dung. Such a position is pointedly avoided here. It is nonsense to believe the notion that wood in particular, or biomass in general, can displace all or most of the other fuels. An industrial economy of the magnitude that we have, if dependent upon wood as a primary fuel, would approach a state described by that Biblical lament, "Woe is me for I am undone." This does not detract, however, from the fact that wood and the other biomass fuels have a very significant part to play in meeting our energy needs. It is a unique part, as the text shows. Given such a disclaimer, we can then ask the question: What is a proper position, a right role, for wood as an energy source?

Wood as an Energy Resource addressed this energy supply topic, first by adopting the philosophy that all supplementary fuels are desirable and should be developed to the maximum extent. That philosophy is adopted because the coal shortage immediately following World War I (which led to riots and deaths), the current petroleum and natural gas shortages causing economic stagnation, and numerous other specific incidents have shown the intellectual and societal bankruptcy of any "few fuels" option, nonrenewable or renewable. The history of Babylon, of Crete, of Greece, and down to that of Nazi Germany confirms that overdependence on one or a few fuels is fraught with peril at all times and ultimately ends up in disaster. Deliberately denying the development of any set of fuel resources is an approach totally devoid of practical value. It is within that frame of reference that the specific evaluation of wood proceeds.

There are numerous specific approaches that can be employed in the analysis of wood as an energy resource. The analytical methods include the technical approach, which examines the biological availability of wood plus the combustion and conversion systems available to use such fuel. Techniques available include an economic assessment dealing with costs of harvesting, combusting, and converting wood materials. A third approach, a comparative approach, also exists. It incorporates elements of the first two analytical methods but treats wood and wood-based materials within the context of the larger family of fuels.

This text adopts that technique and, following comparative analysis, uses wood fuels to examine total energy policy. It traces the historical antecedents of current wood fuel consumption vis-à-vis other fuels, evaluates present use patterns, develops a fuel value analysis of wood, considers the methods best suited for using that fuel, and finally discusses the resources available for increasing the use of the wood energy resource. In all situations it compares wood to coal, oil, and other fuels available.

This organization is somewhat unusual. Traditionally the resource and potential supply issues are dealt with first. Then comes the discussion concerning how to use the fuels in question. The reason for the inversion of topics is this: underlying the text's organization is a time line. The past comes first and is treated as such. The present is the second period discussed. Considerations of fuel value and methods of fuel utilization are issues of the present. The future is, of course, the final period of concern. The potential resource and supply bases are, in the case of wood, more a future concern than a present concern. This organization has the additional advantage of permitting orderly transitions from historical to technical to economic issues.

This discussion of wood fuels, considered so unimportant that federal statistics ignore them, helps place the entire many-fuel option in clearer focus. Through this discussion, roles for other biomass fuels, solar and geothermal energy, hydroelectric power, nuclear power, and by inference the fossil fuels can be posited. The roles put forward here for various fuels offer one man's views of an energy approach with historical, technological, resource, and economic underpinnings.

The research supporting this text included some unique data. *Area Development*, a professional facility planning journal, permitted me to run a questionnaire designed to obtain fuel preference data. It also included questions concerning co-generation. Those results have been included in this presentation. American Fyr-Feeder Engineers provided me access to their files. These new data concerning markets for wood fuel boilers, hence wood fuels, have been included in this book also. Interviews with a host of specialists provided additional insights. These data obtained cover not only wood fuels but also coal, oil, gas, and the entire spectrum of available energy sources.

In developing and presenting a sound role for wood fuel, I relied upon the assistance of many individuals. These were led by Dr. Kyosti V. Sarkanen, who reviewed every word and drawing in the text. His constant comments and suggestions immeasurably aided the research and sharpened the focus of the effort. Several of the formulas and figures employed stemmed directly from his review. Others who helped were Dr. Bernard Blaustein and Dr. Earl T. Hayes, who made significant contributions to the concepts employed. George Voss of American Fyr-Feeder Engineers arranged for the availability of new data from that company's files. Dr. Fred Shafizadeh and James A. Knight provided significant input. William Landers was particularly helpful in reviewing historical data and ideas. Nationiel Guyol lent out-of-print international reports from the 1930s and 1940s, invaluable materials in the overall assessment. Albert Jaeggin, editor of *Area Development*, provided assistance in numerous ways. Additional help came from William Axtman of the American Boiler Manufacturers' Association, Dr. John Zerbe and Dr. John Grantham of the U.S. Forest Service, and Dr. Larry L. Anderson of the University of Utah. Finally, of great assistance was my wife, Millie, who typed every version of this text including the one printed here. Without these people, *Wood as an Energy Resource* could not have been completed. With their aid, its writing has been a very exciting and enjoyable experience. So on to the question: What is a proper position, a right role, of wood fuels?

Chapter 1

A HISTORY OF TRENDS ASSOCIATED WITH FUEL WOOD UTILIZATION

I. INTRODUCTION

That wood and other combustible renewable resources were mankind's first inanimate energy sources, preceding even the use of wind and water power, is well documented. That such combustible fuels exhibited more flexibility than early competitors is also well known. However, the reasons why wood gained initial fuel supremacy, the causes for its decline in both the United States and in other countries, and the historical forces that either promote or constrain its present and future utilization in the energy arena merit examination.

Frequently it is postulated that wood is the fuel of civilization, or the raising of mankind above the level of other primates. Coal is considered the fuel of industrialization. Oil and natural gas are the fuels of advanced industrialization and postindustrial (service) economies. The reasons for such periodic transitions from fuel to fuel, and the role of the declining fuel in the new order, must be understood if the future role of wood among the family of fuels is to be discerned.

In order to make such an analysis, this chapter begins by reviewing the use of wood in the Near East and Europe until 1800 AD, the use of wood as a fuel in the development of the U.S. economy, and finally the use of wood throughout the world

during the first 60 years of the twentieth century. Then, historical forces will be determined as those forces influence the
present and future use of wood as a fuel.

II.   EARLY USE OF FUEL WOOD IN ASIA MINOR AND EUROPE

The control of fire is considered by Kahn and others to be a
cornerstone in human development [1,2]. It achieved acceptance
in both domestic and commercial applications. By about 5400 BC
the smelting of copper and lead with wood and charcoal was being
performed. By 3000 BC the alloying of copper and tin into
bronze in charcoal-fired furnaces was a well-established metal-
lurgical process [3]. Such furnaces, at first, were natural
draft operations. Then slaves were employed to blow air into
the reaction vessel through long reeds and later by operating
foot powered bellows. The use of wind to improve metals smelting and refining was, in that era, yet unknown [4].

Wood thus became the primary fuel for early civilizations.
The island of Cyprus rose to commercial preeminence based upon
this fuel, shipping bronze weapons to the Greek and Roman
armies [4]. The Greek civilization gained much of its commercial
strength from the operation of wood-fueled silver mining and
smelting operations. During this period wood did compete, from
time to time, with alternatives such as bitumen, which was
employed for a time in Babylon [5], or water power as used by
the Roman Empire.

Except for the meeting of requirements for mechanical energy
during the Middle Ages, wood remained the primary fuel employed.
By that time, however, several forces arose that have affected
its utilization ever since. During that period wood-fired
smelters produced iron, copper, lead, and other metals throughout Europe. Wood was also used in the mining and ore concentration activities of metals production. Wood consumption was
high; for example, it required 14 tons of charcoal to smelt one

ton of iron ore [4]. Extensive deforestation resulted from this unbridled consumption in Europe during the fourteenth and fifteenth centuries, causing smelter failures and the design of mobile furnaces [4]. Further, competition for forests and environmental objection to the wood-based metals production caused some southern European states to outlaw mining with its then attendant tree harvesting operations [6].

The experience of England from the end of the Middle Ages until 1800 is particularly instructive in the problems of wood as a fuel, and the transition of industrializing societies away from this energy source. By the end of the Middle Ages, England had a flourishing iron industry in such regions as Weald and the Forest of Dean. But by the 1600s, fuel shortages began to occur. Few woodlots were over 20 acres in size, and in southeastern England there was virtually no fuel wood at all [7]. The number of iron-producing smelters had declined from several hundred to 55, with 26 being distributed between Weald and the Forest of Dean [4]. Trevelyan asserts that this fuel famine caused a decline of English iron production and an international movement of the iron industry to Scandanavia and America, where forests were plentiful. He adds that the scarcity of wood threatened the ability of the island nation to support its increasing population. Many residential dwellings, along with industry, could obtain no fuel at all [8].

These fuel constraints forced England to lead the world in search of new energy sources [9]. Although coal had been mined since the twelfth century, it was the wood shortage that caused that fossil fuel to arise. Abraham Darby learned to produce coke, and substituted it for charcoal successfully in the production of iron in 1709. This event, in Shropshire, England, led to a massive change in that nation's fuel consumption patterns. By 1788, coke-fired blast furnaces outnumbered charcoal-fired vessels by 59 to 26; and by 1809 the ratio was 162 to 11 [10]. It is significant to note, however, that this fuel transition

depended upon the development of a canal transportation network
during the reign of King George III.   This system of canals tied
the nation's economy together and made coal transportation to
inland provinces economical [8].   Thus England's pattern of
industrialization relied upon the development of coal as a
national fuel, and the construction of an efficient national
transportation system.

III.   WOOD AS A FUEL IN THE UNITED STATES

    The pattern of economic and energy development in the United
States differs somewhat from that which occurred in England and
Europe, but many parallels also exist.   Thus, a careful tracing
of fuel utilization in this country elucidates many of the
forces now extant that either promote or constrain the use of
wood as a fuel.   To accomplish this analysis, the following time
periods are used: the U.S. in 1800, 1800-1850, 1850-1870, 1870-
1920, and 1920-1960.   Those periods raise significant issues in
the use of wood as a fuel: issues that will remain of importance
at least for the rest of this century.

A.   *The United States in 1800*

    In order to assess the role of wood as a fuel in the U.S.
at the birth of this nation, it is essential to describe society
at that time.   The use of energy then can be seen, and the use
of wood as a fuel can be established in that context.

    The 1790 census established that the U.S. population, at
that time, was 3.93 million, with only 200,000 or about 5%
living in urban areas [11].   Only 3% of the labor force gained
employment in manufacturing, while 82.6% worked in agriculture [11].   It was, in short, a capital-short and labor-short
economy, which substituted land and the products of the land
for capital and labor wherever possible [9].

The transportation system at that time consisted primarily
of seaborne commerce. Overland transport consisted of rough
turnpikes, and overland shipment was most expensive. Bruchey
places the cost at $0.30-0.70/ton mile [11], a prohibitive rate
for bulk commodities such as fuel.

Given such a situation one can easily see why the family
remained the principal production unit, and why manufacturing
operations were small, designed for serving local markets. At
that time no national market existed. Manufactured goods
included iron and iron products, paper (based upon rags as the
raw material), and other essential commodities.

The economy of 1800 overwhelmingly favored the use of wood
as a fuel. It could be obtained readily for domestic purposes
and had to be cut anyway, if land was to be cleared for agricultural purposes. The dispersion of the iron industry in small
units, permitted charcoal consumption, and the large wood
requirement of charcoal-fired iron producers reinforced this
diffuse nature of the industry [9]. Thus iron was produced,
principally for stoves, in such places as Saugus, Massachusetts,
and Peterborough, New Hampshire [12]. Wood, then, was used
unless mechanical energy for operating sawmills or grinding
flour was required. Coal was all but unknown at that time.

B. *The U.S. Economy, 1800-1850*

The U.S. economy, in the first 50 years of the nineteenth
century, laid the foundation for industrialization. This preindustrial era also set in motion forces that would cause the
ultimate shift of the economy from wood to coal and other fuels.

During this 50-year span, the U.S. population grew to over
15 million persons. Fully one-third of these people lived west
of the Appalachians. The percentage of the population living in
cities rose to over 10%, and the percentage of workers employed
in agriculture declined to about 60%, while those in

manufacturing approached 10% [11]. The value added by agriculture dropped to 60%, while the value added by manufacturing more
than doubled, rising to 30%. Mining and construction remained
stable [11].

Those gross statistics only suggest the underlying forces in
economic organization. The agricultural sector shifted from
subsistence to commercial farming. Francis L. Lowell introduced
the factory system for textile manufacturing. That 1814 development in Waltham, Massachusetts, introduced the pattern of industrial organization that was to be adopted widely in succeeding
years [13]. During these years stationary steam engines,
primarily fired by wood, were introduced into industrial practice [14]. Steam power complemented water and wind power in
providing mechanical energy to manufacturing plants. One example
of its deployment is the early Maine lumber industry where,
between 1820 and 1850, 36 steam-powered mills were built [15].

The transportation revolution began in this period, a
development essential to undergird industrial development. The
Erie Canal opened in the 1820s, symbolizing a canal-building era.
Steam boats began plying the inland waterways. In 1817, riverboat shipments were only 3290 tons, but by 1840 some 536 such
vessels were carrying 82,600 tons of cargo annually [11]. The
railroad system, initiated in 1830, grew to 9000 miles of track
by 1850 [16].

Although wood was not the primary industrial energy source,
it remained the dominant fuel for the nation as a whole in this
era. Wind and water power were employed by the majority of
manufacturers. However wood was the primary transportation fuel.
The combination of available waterways and abundant supplies of
cordwood were the causes for riverboat success [9]. Railroads
were also fueled by wood, as illustrated by Fig. 1. Their
initial success depended upon its availability [17]. Wood also
supplied 90% of the fuel used in home heating and cooking
applications [18].

FIGURE 1. *Early wood-fired locomotive on display at the Smithsonian Museum of History and Technology, Washington, D.C.*

Wood continued to dominate, perhaps because it remained cheaper than the combustible fuel alternatives, anthracite and bituminous coal. The cost and consumption of fuels in Philadelphia, ca. 1825, demonstrates this fact. Table I presents the comparative price advantage of wood. It also shows that coal was rapidly becoming cost competitive.

Despite the high cost of charcoal, the charcoal iron industry expanded during this period. It was the final halcyon days of that industry. If the Hopewell, Pennsylvania, furnace is any example, the decade 1830–1840 was the high point, when long periods of production and profit were experienced [19]. By this period, charcoal iron producers had learned tree crop rotation at a rudimentary level. New Jersey iron industry practice was for one furnace to own 20,000 acres of timber, and to harvest

8 1 Trends Associated with Fuel Wood Utilization

TABLE I

The Cost and Consumption of Fuels in Philadelphia, ca. 1825 [18]

Fuel	Cost ($/10^6 Btu)	Consumption (in 10^{12} Btu)
Wood	0.22	2.80
Anthracite	0.25	0.72
Bituminous coal	0.29	0.13
Charcoal	0.41	0.07

1000 acres annually. In Pennsylvania, several furnaces were
supported by over 8000 acres of company-owned woodland, and iron
makers there also harvested on a rotation basis [19]. Such large
wood-producing areas were necessary, because it required 6000
cords of wood (160,000 bushels of charcoal) to produce 1000 tons
of iron [19].

As the prices in Table I suggest, however, the charcoal iron
industry was beginning to experience economic difficulties due
to the high cost of operation and, in some cases, resource
insufficiency. Almost 62% of the cost of making such iron was
in the cost of obtaining wood, and converting it into the ore
reductant [19]. While cost remained a key problem, forest
depletion did close several forges [19]. Finally, the opening
of anthracite and bituminous coal fields in the 1830s heralded
a fuel switch similar to the one that occurred in England during
the previous century [11]. In 1836 the Pennsylvania Legislature
authorized the formation of corporations to make iron with coke
and in 1838 it authorized similar corporations to employ anthracite. By 1850 anthracite iron enjoyed a 490% cost advantage
over charcoal iron. Thus, by 1850 there were 100 anthracite
furnaces and 103 charcoal furnaces in Pennsylvania [19] in
addition to the iron production units based on Connellsville
coke.

In the preindustrial years then, wood enjoyed a commanding lead over other fuels. This lead was threatened, however, by the incipient industrialization, the beginning of a coal industry, and the nascent urbanization of the population.

C. The Period of Transition, 1850-1870

The twenty years 1850-1870 witnesses political and economic activities that would tear the nation apart, tie it together, and set the stage for rapid industrialization. During this period fuel wood utilization peaked, coal production and consumption increased dramatically, commercial petroleum production began in Titusville, Pennsylvania, and total energy usage almost doubled.

In 1860 an economic profile shows that the leading industries were cotton goods, lumber, boots and shoes, flour and meal, men's clothing, iron, machinery, woolen goods, wagons, and leather goods. Of these, textiles and apparel supplied 50% of the value added by manufacture with lumbering supplying 14.3% [11].

The U.S. had produced the most advanced timber-working technology in the world [9], and events occurring during this period served to enhance the growth of this nation's forest industries. The mechanical pulping process, invented in Germany in 1844, was commercially applied in Pennsylvania in 1867. The soda pulping process, invented in England in 1851, was applied in the U.S. in 1855. The sulfite process, which was invented in the U.S. in 1866, was commercially installed in 1867 [20]. These processes had vast importance for the next economic era. They permitted the paper industry to shift its raw material base from rags to wood, particularly during the last 30 years of the nineteenth century.

The Civil War played a significant role in this economic development. Graebner, et al. [13] observe that it accomplished the following: established a base for productive facilities,

established a base for capital formation, and created a political
climate dominated by industrial interests.

Transportation and communication improvements occurred apace.
In 1855, the St. Mary's Canal connecting Lake Superior and Lake
Huron was completed, facilitating bulk movement of iron ore to
production centers.   In 1865, Samuel Van Cycle built the first
oil pipeline.   In 1869, the transcontinental railroad became an
operating reality [16].   These events, plus the more than doubling of railroad trackage in the U.S. exerted considerable
pressure on the economy to industrialize.   This pressure forced
changes in fuel utilization patterns.

While all fuels were used in increasing amounts during this
period, wood lost significant ground on a proportional basis.
This trend was particularly pronounced in the industrial arena,
where coal assumed the lead over all renewable resources.
Table II illustrates the shift of industry from renewable to
nonrenewable resources in the transition period.

TABLE II

Industrial Fuel Consumption, 1850-1870 [18]

Energy source	Industrial energy supply (%)		
	1850	1860	1870
Coal	19.4	30.5	57.7
Water	25.0	22.0	20.0
Wind	38.8	35.6	12.9
Wood	16.7	11.9	9.4

The transportation industry continued to rely upon wood and, as rail emerged victorious over water transportation, it assumed the lead in fuel wood consumption for transportation purposes. By 1860 railroads were consuming 6 million cords of wood to 3 million cords for steamboats [18]. The transportation industry, however, was beginning to shift to coal. By 1865, about 25% of railroad energy was supplied by this fossil fuel [18]. The iron industry, during this period, became dominated by coal-fueled operations; at the same time, however, the absolute demand for iron during the Civil War propped up the declining charcoal industry [19].

It can be seen then that the surge of manufacturing activity brought on the use of coal as the dominant industrial fuel. Further, this transition to industrialization created conditions that began to force wood out of several energy markets it was holding: particularly in the metal and transportation sectors. Only the residential market remained secure.

D. *The Period of Industrial Development, 1870-1920*

The 50 years 1870-1920 were remarkable in their execution of total social change within the United States. Industrial, transportation, consumption, and conservation developments occurred at an incredible pace. These developments exerted a profound influence on energy consumption patterns, exacerbating the problems plaguing the fuel wood industry. While total population increased, the urban population rose from 9.9 million to over 47 million, and urban land area rose from under 2 million acres to almost 8 million acres [21]. The urban population became virtually equal to the rural population. More significantly, in 1870, the value added by all industry was 43% and the value added by agriculture was 57% of total value added by production processes. By 1900 the ratio was 65:35 [11].

Within the total industrial community, massive changes occurred. Andrew Carnegie introduced the Bessemer process in steelmaking, creating a need for and the advantages of large production units [11]. U.S. Steel became large enough to build its own city, Gary, Indiana, for the expansion of capacity. By the end of this period, 20 of today's 100 largest corporations were formed [11]. Production of all manufactured products rose dramatically.

The period 1870–1920 was, both technically and economically, one of the most explosive for the pulp and paper industry. Similarly it was an expansive period for lumber production. In the pulp and paper industry, the Kraft process was invented in Germany in 1884 and introduced into the U.S. shortly thereafter. The first installation was at the Halifax Paper Co. of North Carolina. The development of this process has had more influence on modern papermaking than any other process [20]. The introduction of Kraft pulping, plus the momentum gained by the pulping processes introduced during the transition period, brought U.S. pulp production from 1000 tons to over 3.5 million tons between 1869 and 1919. By 1920 pulp production reached 3.8 million tons and paper production reached 7.2 million tons, as Table III shows. During this period lumber production also rose from 12.8×10^6 to 34.6×10^6 bd ft [22]. The combined growth of these two industries forced the harvest of wood used in the materials industries to exceed the harvest of wood for fuel purposes.

The transportation story is equivalent to the railroad story. In 1870, there were only about 50,000 miles of railroad lines, but 30 years later there were 150,000 miles of track [23]. In one decade, 1970–1880, almost 41,000 miles of track were built [23]. This growth in trackage, coupled with markedly declining costs of rail transportation, encouraged interregional shipment of bulky commodities [24]. Thus Bruchey concludes that between 1870 and 1900 the railraods were responsible for the

TABLE III

The Growth of Pulp and Paper Industries, 1869-1920[a]

Year	Wood pulp production	Paper and paperboard production
1869	1	386
1879	23	452
1889	306	935
1899	1180	2168
1909	2496	4121
1919	3518	5966
1920	3822	7185

[a]In 10^3 tons. Data from Hair [22].

creation of a national mass market in the U.S. [11]. Finally, the U.S. was one national economy rather than an assemblage of regional economies.

The creation of a national unified economic structure brought dramatic changes in fuel consumption led by the domination of coal, the rise of petroleum, and the introduction of both natural gas and hydroelectric power. Wood suffered on both an absolute and relative basis, losing its transportation and iron markets totally [9], and losing part of its residential market. Table IV traces this shift in national energy consumption patterns.

Three factors, more than any others, influenced this decline of wood as a fuel. The dramatic rise of forest products industries, as exemplified by paper (but also experienced by lumber), created large and higher value demands for the majority of wood harvested. The tying together of a national economy created a national energy market. Since wood is basically a locally marketed fuel, the creation of a national energy market can be considered a critical constraint on its utilization.

TABLE IV

U.S. Energy Consumption, 1870-1920[a]

	Fuel				
Year	Wood	Coal	Petroleum	Natural gas	Hydro-electric power
1870	2.9	1.0	-	-	-
1880	2.9	2.0	0.1	-	-
1890	2.5	4.1	0.2	0.3	-
1900	2.0	6.8	0.2	0.3	0.3
1910	1.9	12.7	1.0	0.5	0.5
1920	1.6	15.5	2.6	0.8	0.8

[a]In 10^{15} Btu. Data from Enzer et al. [25].

Finally, the absolute energy requirement in 1910, 16.6×10^{15} Btu and in 1920, 21.3×10^{15} Btu made the continued domination of wood impossible. In 1920, meeting that demand would have required the harvesting of over a billion cords of fuel wood.

The enumeration of those three forces presents a simple, succinct explanation of the forces behind the transition from wood to coal. More complex trends associated with this transition have been identified by Berg [26]. The fuel using industries modified their processes to capitalize upon the higher energy value and uniformity of coal (as compared to wood). Industries making such modifications included steel and glass. Further, the coal industry attracted a host of innovative technicians who advanced coal utilization technology at a rapid pace. Berg asserts that the wood fuel industry did not marshall a similar technical force, and thus fell behind in the technological arena. This latter assertion is not without contradiction, however. Despite the somewhat controversial nature of the

technological talent argument, Berg's point remains intact. Coal
did benefit from rapid technological advances which supported
the economic transition away from wood fuels.

As a final note, the environmental protection movement began
in this period. Following on the 1864 publication of Man and
Nature, written by George Perkins Marsh, California set aside a
small portion of Yosemite Valley as a state park. In 1872, the
Yellowstone Act created that national park and established a
precedent for land withdrawals to support recreational activity
[27]. In 1891, the U.S. Forest Reserves, now called National
Forests, were established. Gifford Pinchot's leadership was
highly evident in this time period, for his vigorous action aided
in the development of such practices. The conservation movement
had no real influence on fuel wood production at the beginning
of the twentieth century, but its modern extension could have
serious implications by the end of this century.

E. The Period of Advanced Industrialization, 1920-1960

The demographic and economic trends from 1920 to 1960 are
well known. The industrial economy consolidated its gains. The
transportation system added automobiles, trucks, and airplanes
to its array of transport methods. The environmental/
conservation movement grew more powerful and more strident.

A new trend also rose: competition for forest land to meet
the housing, recreation, and transportation needs of city
dwellers. As Table V shows, city land rose from 10 to 17 million
acres, recreational land rose from 13 to 60 million acres, transportation land increased from 23 to 25 million acres, and
commercial forest land declined from 500 to 484 acres. The land
committed to recreation and wilderness, as a percentage of the
land committed to commercial forests, rose substantially
between 1920 and 1950. In one short period, 1945-1953, 70,000
acres of commercial forest land were withdrawn from timber

TABLE V

Selected Land Use Patterns in the U.S., 1920-1950[a]

Selected land use	Area employed (in 10^6 acres)			
	1920	1930	1940	1950
Cities	10	12	13	17
Public relations (except city parks)	12	15	41	46
Wildlife and wilderness	1	1	12	14
Transportation	23	24	24	25
Commercial forests	500	495	488	484
Total U.S. land	1904	1904	1904	1904

[a]Data from Lansberg et al. [21].

production annually in Washington and Oregon. These acres were converted into such land uses as transmission line right-of-ways, roads, dams, and air fields [28]. For the first time, the forest industries had to compete with other interests for the productive land itself. As with the conservation trend, which appears as part of this force, the implications for the future are more significant than for the period in which the trend emerged.

Fuel utilization within industry was also changing rapidly, and these trends created radical shifts in the use of wood-based fuel. The agricultural sector abandoned the use of draft animals in favor of petroleum-fueled tractors, and liquid fuels commanded increasing proportions of the transportation industry as well [29]. All industries became more energy intensive, substituting plentiful fossil fuels for relatively scarce labor. This rise in energy intensity led to dramatic changes in fuel consumption patterns in wood fuel utilization systems and in the petrochemical and plastics industries.

The paper industry demonstrates the changes in production systems and fuel utilization patterns. During this period, kraft pulping assumed a dominant position in the paper industry. The kraft process, more than any other development, led to the rapid rise of the southern pulp industry. In other regions its successful application to hemlock in the 1920s created a use for that otherwise bypassed tree. Thus the kraft process was at the root of the development of the Pacific Northwest paper industry [30]. The kraft process was used in the production of nearly 60% of the pulp manufactured in 1960 [20]. At the same time, semichemical pulping was introduced as a means for converting byproduct hardwood chips into paper. After its commercial introduction in 1925, semichemical rose to fourth place among pulp-making processes [20]. Total paper production rose from 7.5 to 40 million tons annually during this period. The paper industry became the ninth largest manufacturing industry in the U.S., the seventh largest industrial consumer of energy, the largest industrial consumer of fuel oil, and also the largest self-generator of energy, the latter fact being based upon wood and wood waste [20].

The paper industry's appetite for fuel oil reflected the energy consumption patterns of the nation as a whole. Table VI, an extension of Table IV, shows this continued national shift away from wood to fossil fuels. However, by this period, the shift was away from solid fuels including coal to liquid and gaseous fuels and to electricity.

Not only was the U.S. economy turning to oil and natural gas, but it was also expanding its fuel options. No longer was the selection limited to wind, water, or wood. Several general fuels existed. Further, the economy was showing the capability of handling fuels useful for special purposes (e.g., nuclear power for electricity generation). In addition, industries such as sugar refining were relying upon their wastes.

TABLE VI

Energy Consumption in the U.S., 1920-1960[a]

Year	Fuel				
	Wood	Coal	Petro-leum	Natural gas	Hydro-electric power
1920	1.6	15.5	2.6	0.8	0.8
1930	1.5	13.6	5.4	2.0	0.8
1940	1.4	12.5	7.5	2.7	0.9
1950	1.2	12.9	13.5	6.2	1.4
1960	0.3[b]	10.1	20.1	12.7	1.7

[a]*In 10^{15} Btu. Data from Lansberg et al. [25].*

[b]*This extrapolation is based upon United Nations data reported by Guyol (see reference 40); no official national figures given. It should be noted that this number does not include spent pulping liquor. If that wood fuel is included, the total is closer to 0.75 quads.*

Within the wood fuel arena, a transformation was taking place that laid the foundation for its present resurgence. By the 1920s the demand for forest products was such that those industries were commanding 67% of the wood harvested [31]. The remaining 33%, fuel wood, was used residentially. A small resurgence in residential wood fuel use during that decade caused construction of new factories producing wood-fired stoves for such home heating applications [12]. But the major revolution was the introduction of wood waste as a fuel. Residential and light commercial sawdust burners began appearing in about 1925 [32]. They caught on quickly and, by 1930, 6300 homes in Portland, Oregon, and 3800 homes in Seattle, Washington, were fueled with sawdust. Such waste was supplying 56×10^{12} Btu

annually to homes in the Pacific Northwest by 1930 [33]. The
use of such wood waste as an energy source was also common practice in the forest products industry.

Perhaps one of the better symbols of the switch from harvested wood to fuel wood, and certainly a most ironic example, is
that of the Ford Motor Co. That company, which did so much to
increase the usage of petroleum, installed a 400-ton per day wood
waste pyrolysis plant at its Iron Mountain, Michigan, plant in
1924. Half of the feed material came from the company's sawmill and the other half came from its body plant. The installation was a Stafford-Badger continuous vertical retort system,
which daily produced 120 tons of charcoal for outside sale,
2×10^6 ft^3 of producer gas used in company boilers, 5800 gallons
of ethyl acetate used in the company to make lacquer, and 3800
gallons of other chemicals for sale to other firms. It was at
that time the largest pyrolysis installation built and
operated [34].

A less arcane, but more substantial, example of developing
waste-based fuel systems is the emergence of the black liquor
recovery furnace. George H. Tomlinson installed the first
stationary recovery furnace in 1926, at Cornwall, Ontario. This
furnace incorporated energy recovery into the design: a concept
that was novel at that time. The first furnaces were somewhat
unreliable, and the paper mill installed three in order to have
one running at any given time. During the 1930s, with assistance
from Babcock and Wilcox Co., the Tomlinson system of energy and
chemicals recovery was perfected [35].

This stationary furnace competed about evenly with rotary
furnace designs, which by the 1930s also incorporated energy
recovery. Combustion Engineering Co., the second boiler maker
involved in black liquor recovery systems, was committed to the
latter approach. During the period 1936-1938, the company moved
into the stationary furnace field, introducing significant
improvements to the Tomlinson design. The work of Combustion

Engineering, combined with the pioneering of Tomlinson and
Babcock and Wilcox, led to the design of the modern stationary
spent liquor recovery system. By the 1940s and 1950s, Tomlinson-
type furnaces became common equipment in the kraft pulp and paper
industry. Its ubiquity in pulp and paper resulted not only from
efficiency considerations, but also from scale-up limitations
facing rotary furnace designs [36].

While the economy in general was shifting away from its use
of wood as fuel, even more dramatic events were occurring in the
chemical industry. Until this century the wood-based naval
stores industry producing turpentine, resin, rosin, and a variety
of other products was the primary element of the chemicals
industry [3,6]. Products of wood distillation such as methanol,
acetone, and acetate were also important in the chemicals industry. In the period 1916-1921, dissolving pulp processes began
to emerge. These processes provided the technology base for
rayon and cellophane, and a host of other synthetic materials.
Production of dissolving pulp rose to about 2 million tons and
stabilized at that level [37].

While wood was increasing its absolute contribution, the
more concentrated fossil fuels emerged as the preeminent
suppliers of chemicals and plastics. In some instances they
displaced wood, but in most cases they opened up new markets for
synthetics. Natural gas replaced wood as the primary raw
material for acetone production in 1926, and similarly replaced
wood in methanol production in 1930 [33]. The total shift in
plastics, illustrated in Fig. 2, came in the 1940s and 1950s and
was based upon the ability of petrochemical firms to vertically
integrate backwards into oil production, and their ability to
achieve massive economies of scale, substituting capital for
labor [38].

By 1960 then, wood had lost its traditional fuel markets -
including most of its residential market - to the more concentrated fossil fuels and to electricity. It had also lost some

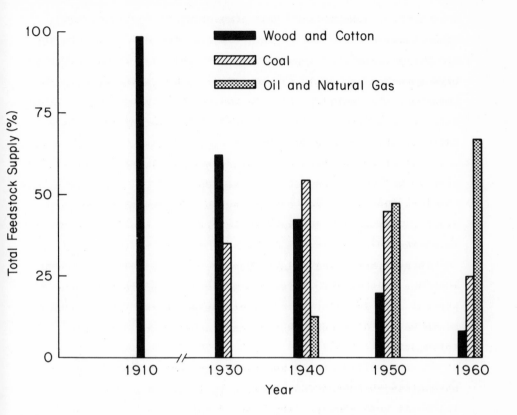

FIGURE 2.   The relative importance of selected feedstocks
for plastics manufacturing [38].   Adapted from National Materials
Advisory Board, Problems and Legislative Opportunities in the
Basic Materials Industries, National Academy of Science/
National Academy of Engineering, Washington, D.C., 1975.

of its plastics applications, retaining those markets where
special properties mandated its use. Petroleum-based plastics,
on the other hand, found a host of new applications, which permitted them to dominate the industry. Wood as a raw material was
increasingly restricted to use in the forest products industries,
where growing demand for this fiber source consumed almost all of
the trees that were harvested.

IV.   INTERNATIONAL USE OF FUEL WOOD IN THE TWENTIETH CENTURY

For a variety of reasons, the U.S. experience may be considered somewhat atypical. These reasons include the combination of advanced industrialization plus the ready availability of all types of domestic fossil fuels during the process of industrialization. This combination has not occurred elwewhere. Because this situation has been unique, and because it no longer exists particularly with respect to an abundance of oil and natural gas, the experience of other nations during the twentieth century is particularly useful in examining the role of wood within the total family of fuels.

International analysis is hampered by a paucity of good data. Thus one is forced to rely upon a few selected reports, and to present data in relative and comparative terms. Such techniques minimize the difficulties inherent in using the available information.[1]

As the world entered the twentieth century, almost every nation used wood and wood derived fuels to some extent. As Table VII demonstrates, some 65% of the nations in the world depended upon wood for more than 10% of their energy in 1937. Among the world community, 46% of the nations obtained more than 25% of their energy from wood in that year, and 24% obtained more than half of their energy from harvesting available forests [39]. In that year, developed nations consumed 66.7% of all wood fuel, and less developed nations consumed 33.3% of the wood-based fuels. The division was 4.2 and 2.1×10^{15} Btu, respectively. Yet as Table VII shows, absolute consumption and relative importance were far from equal in 1937.

---

[1]*This problem stems from the fact that wood is a noncommercial fuel that is often harvested and used without entering the channels of trade. Thus data gathering itself can only be accomplished by rough estimation.*

TABLE VII

Consumption of Wood Fuel in 1937[a]

	Number	Total energy budget (%)	Mean national energy budget (in 10^{15} Btu)
Countries using wood for 50-100% of energy	31	24	0.05
Countries using wood for 25-50% of energy	30	23	0.10
Countries using wood for 10-25% of energy	23	18	0.38
Countries using wood for <10% of energy	45	35	1.00
Total	130	100	0.42

[a]Data from *Energy Resources of the World* [40].

While most of the nations that obtained less than 10% of their energy from wood were undeveloped, several were not. Of the 15 countries, in that year, with energy budgets exceeding one quad, 8 obtained less than 10% of their fuel from wood and 7 obtained between 10 and 25% from wood. No large energy-consuming nation obtained more than 25% of its fuel from wood. Also it should be noted that, among the largest energy consumers, the USSR was most dependent upon wood, obtaining 17% of its energy from this source [40]. During the early and mid 1920s, after the Russian Revolution, that country was over 50% dependent upon wood. This short, abnormally high dependence upon wood fuel resulted from absolute unavailability of fossil fuels rather than increased wood consumption. Total energy use declined, and thus the apparent position of wood improved as it was the "emergency" fuel [41].

By 1949, the distribution of wood fuel consumption had changed substantially, with developed nations using 59% of the total consumed, and developing nations using 41% [42]. Total consumption of wood fuel had risen to some 7.2 quads, with 1.3 quads being supplied by lumber mill wastes [42]. This use of lumber mill waste was most pronounced in North America, where 33% of the wood fuel consumed came from such sources.

The 12-year trends from 1937 to 1949 completely mask the temporary dramatic increase in wood as a fuel throughout Europe during World War II. Egon Glesinger, in the classic book The Coming Age of Wood, describes how the Swedish economy was converted almost totally to wood fuel during those years in the absence of coal and other fossil fuels. Motor vehicles employed wood gas generators to provide fuel, and stationary gas generators produced town gas. By the end of the war, half of that nation's automotive population was in service. Homes had not gone cold. A tripling of fuel wood production combined with careful planning kept the essential industries and services functioning smoothly [43]. The prominence of wood fuel and the ubiquity of wood gas generators throughout Europe during World War II can be seen from the number of such converters in operation. France had some 100,000 in use, Germany had 150,000 wood gas generators on trucks and 30,000 on tractors, and Switzerland had 15,000 portable wood gasifiers for motor vehicles. Glesinger observes that at least 10,000 units were in service in every European country [43]. Wood was the certain, domestically available, emergency fuel.

Again, postwar emergency conditions forced unusually high wood consumption in certain countries. In Japan, during the immediate postwar period, wood supplied over 50% of the total energy consumed [41]. As with Russia of the World War I, drastic

conditions existed, which precluded the use of fossil fuels in
quantities anywhere near normal quantities.

By the period 1960–1962, world consumption of wood for fuel
had risen to 8.2 quads [43]. The trends from 1937 to ca. 1971
are summarized in Table VIII. It is clear that, in the final
12 years presented, two dramatic changes occurred: there was a
drastic decline of wood fuel utilization in North America and an
equally dramatic increase in fuel wood consumption in Asia. The
American situation may be partially explained by the rapid rise
in the utilization of artificially low priced natural gas. One
can speculate that the constant state of war that has existed in
Asia from World War II until the present day, contributed significantly to the doubling of fuel wood consumption there. Those
North American and Asian trends, in reality, were the cutting
edge of larger forces. The developed nations were, en masse,
moving to oil rapidly and reducing fuel wood consumption. The

TABLE VIII

World Wood Fuel Consumption Trends: 1937-1960

Continent/region	Fuel wood consumption (in 10^{15} Btu)		
	1937[a]	1949[b]	1960-1962[c]
North America	1.64	2.05	0.35
Latin America	0.55	1.02	1.44
Europe	1.06	1.32	0.81
USSR	0.92	0.75	0.76
Asia	1.26	1.30	3.44
Africa	0.89	0.78	1.37
Total	6.32	7.22	8.17

[a]From Guyol [40].   [b]From UN [42].   [c]FAO [44].

developing nations, under pressures of population growth, new-
found nationalism, and periodic conflict, were turning more and
more to fuel wood. By 1960-1962, the developed nations were
consuming less than half of the wood fuel used in the world.

V.   THE FORCES OF HISTORY

Certainly the history of wood consumption as fuel defines
trends and forces, now extant, that promote or constrain its
continued use as a fuel in the United States and in the world.
These forces will become significant in developing the broad
outlines of the forecast of wood consumption for energy purposes
in the U.S., during the last part of this century (Chapter 8).
Despite the single-nation focus of those projections, experiences
throughout the world have significance in identifying the forces
articulated below.

Of primary importance is the fact that, for the long term,
wood has never sustained a broad national industrialized
economy. When such an economy emerges, linked together by an
efficient transportation system and demanding large absolute
quantities of fuel, wood gives way to coal and oil. This experience, illustrated previously for both England and the U.S., has
occurred repeatedly. Statistically it is demonstrated by the
declining reliance on fuel as national energy budgets rise. It
results from the fact that wood is basically a local fuel.

A corollary parameter to the first one described is that,
in an industrial economy, wood is too valuable to be harvested
and sold as a fuel. The decline in the use of wood as fuel in
the U.S. and the rise in production of paper, plywood, and
lumber have marched in lockstep. Further, Glesinger places the
1949 relative values at $4/ton for fuel wood and $50-150/ton
when converted into materials [43]. Since that gap has not been
reduced appreciably, the situation he describes remains in
force.

A third force that developed, not unrelated to the second, was that some land became more valuable, economically or politically, for uses other than timber production. These uses included housing, transportation, recreation, and conservation. Such competition for land continues unabated, and it impinges upon unfettered use of the forest as a system for producing material and energy products. Since the U.S. population continues to increase in size, degree of urbanization, and affluence, this trend can only continue to increase in intensity.

While the first three parameters suggest that wood, as a fuel, has limited future utility at best, there are other factors promoting its utilization. It has excellent utility in special situations, particularly where synergistic forces promote its application. In the early years of this nation, the need to clear land for agriculture made wood partially a byproduct of development - and improved its competitive position. During the 1920s, the development of wood waste-to-fuel systems suggested an emerging synergy between waste disposal and fuel production. The Tomlinson furnace offers a synergy between chemical recovery and energy recovery. That such synergistic forces were temporarily disrupted by cheap natural gas does not diminish their importance. Energy technologies have been developed, increasingly, to handle such supplementary fuels in the U.S. Thus such synergistic fuels may enjoy competitive advantages in the future.

Wood is also a useful fuel in special or emergency situations where no other energy source is readily available locally or nationally. Careful husbanding of renewable resources can perpetuate such energy contribution for extended periods of time if necessary.

In summary then, wood and wood-based materials have become special-purpose rather than universal fuels. While wood was perhaps civilization's first inanimate energy source, it has

given up its ubiquity to the more concentrated fossil fuels,
coal and oil. It has retained applicability in those circumstances where local conditions or events dictate.

REFERENCES

1. Herman Kahn et al., The Next 200 Years. New York: William
    Morrow (for the Hudson Institute), 1976.
2. Fred Shafizadeh and William F. DeGroot, Combustion charac-
    teristics of cellulosic fuels, in Thermal Uses and
    Properties of Carbohydrates and Lignins (F. Shafizadeh,
    K. Sarkanen, and D. Tillman, eds.). New York: Academic
    Press, 1976.
3. The Last Two Million Years. New York: The Readers Digest
    Assn., 1973.
4. H. G. Cordero and L. H. Tarring, From Babylon to Birmingham.
    London, England: Quinn Press, 1960.
5. David Cass-Beggs, Energy and civilization, Proc. Int.
    Biomass Energy Conf. Winnipeg, Canada: Biomass Energy
    Institute, May 13-15, 1973.
6. Agricola, De Re Metallica (Hoover translation).
7. Charles F. Carroll, The forest society of New England, in
    America's Wooden Age (Brooke Hindle, ed.). Tarrytown,
    New York: Sleepy Hollow Restorations, 1975.
8. G. M. Trevelyan, History of England, Vol. III. Garden City,
    New York: Doubleday, 1953.
9. Nathan Rosenberg, Technology and American Economic Growth.
    New York: Harper and Row, 1972.
10. T. S. Ashton, Iron and Steel in the Industrial Revolution.
    Manchester: Manchester Univ. Press, 1924.
11. Stuart Bruchey, Growth of the Modern American Economy.
    New York: Dodd, Mead, 1975.

12. Charles J. Jordan and Jessie S. Cole, The shape of things to come, _Yankee_, January 1974.

13. Norman A. Graebner, Gilbert C. Fite, and Philip L. White, _A History of the American People_, Vol. I. New York: McGraw-Hill, 1971.

14. Louis C. Hunter, Water power in the century of the steam engine, in _America's Wooden Age: Aspects of Its Early Technology_ (Brooke Hindle, ed.). Tarrytown, New York: Sleepy Hollow Restorations, 1975.

15. Philip T. Coolidge, _History of the Maine Woods_. Bangor, Maine: Philip T. Coolidge, 1963.

16. Howard Mumford Jones, _The Age of Energy_. New York: Viking, 1970.

17. Brooke Hindle, The span of the wooden age, in _America's Wooden Age: Aspects of Its Early Technology_ (Brooke Hindle, ed.). Tarrytown, New York: Sleepy Hollow Restorations, 1975.

18. Sam H. Schurr and Bruce C. Netschert, _Energy in the American Economy, 1850–1975_. Baltimore: Johns Hopkins Univ. Press (for Resources for the Future, Inc.), 1960.

19. Joseph E. Walker, _Hopewell Village: The Dynamics of a Nineteenth Century Iron-Making Community_. Philadelphia: Univ. of Pennsylvania Press, 1966.

20. C. E. Libby, History of pulp and paper, in _Pulp and Paper Science and Technology_, Vol. I. New York: McGraw-Hill, 1962.

21. Hans H. Lansberg, Leonard L. Fishman, and Joseph L. Fisher, _Resources in America's Future_. Baltimore: Johns Hopkins Univ. Press, 1963.

22. Dwight Hair, _Historical Forestry Statistics of the United States_. Washington, D.C.: U.S. Dept. of Agriculture, 1958.

23. Woodrow Wilson, _A History of the American People_, Vol. V. New York: Harper and Bros., 1901.

24. Jeffrey G. Williamson, The railroads and midwestern development 1870–1890: A general equilibrium history, in Essays in Nineteenth Century Economic History (David C. Klingaman and Richard K. Vedder, eds.). Athens, Ohio: Ohio Univ. Press, 1975.

25. Herman Enzer, Walter Dupree, and Stanley Miller, Energy Perspectives: A Presentation of Major Energy and Energy Related Data. Washington, D.C.: U.S. Dept. of the Interior, 1975.

26. Charles A. Berg, Process innovation and changes in industrial energy use, Science, 199, No. 432, Feb. 10, 1978.

27. America 200: The Legacy of Our Lands. Washington, D.C.: U.S. Dept. of Interior, 1976.

28. C. Montgomery Johnson, People, trees, and directions, in Proc. Wood Industries Conf. Am. Inst. Chem. Eng., Sept. 10–12, 1959.

29. John W. Frey and H. Chandler Ide, eds. A History of the Petroleum Administration for War. Washington, D.C.: USGPO, 1946.

30. Murray C. Morgan, The Last Wilderness. Seattle: Univ. of Washington Press, 1955.

31. Leonard Fishman, Future demand for forest resources, in Forest Policy for the Future (Marion Clawson, ed.). Washington, D.C.: Resources for the Future, Inc., June, 1974.

32. E. C. Wiley, Rating and care of domestic sawdust burners, Bull. Ser., No. 15, Engineering Station, Oregon State College, June, 1941.

33. Henry K. Benson, Chemical Utilization of Wood. Washington, D.C.: USGPO, 1932.

34. W. G. Nelson, Waste-wood utilization by the Badger-Stafford process, Ind. Eng. Chem. 22, No. 4, April, 1930.

35. G. H. Tomlinson II, Black liquor recovery--an historical note, Forum on Kraft Recovery Alternatives. Appleton, Wisconsin: The Institute of Paper Chemistry, April, 1976.

36. Thomas M. Grace, Perspectives on recovery technology, Forum on Kraft Recovery Alternatives. Appleton, Wisconsin: The Institute of Paper Chemistry, April, 1976.

37. Peter Koch, Utilization of Southern Pines, Vol. II Agricultural Handbook, No. 420. Washington, D.C.: USGPO, 1972.

38. Albert V. G. Hahn, The Petrochemical Industry. New York: McGraw-Hill, 1970.

39. National Materials Advisory Board, Problems and Legislative Opportunities in the Basic Materials Industries. Washington, D.C.: Nat. Acad. Sci., 1975.

40. Nathaniel Guyol, Energy Resources of the World, Dept. of State Publication 3428. Washington, D.C.: USGPO, 1949.

41. Hans Thirring, Energy for Man (1976 ed.). New York: Harper, 1956.

42. World Energy Supplies in Selected Years, 1929-1950. Publ. Ser. J., No. 1. New York: Statistical Office of the United Nations.

43. Egon Glesinger, The Coming Age of Wood. New York: Simon and Schuster, 1949.

44. Food and Agricultural Organization of the United Nations (FAO), Wood World's Trends and Prospects, Basic Study No. 16, Rome, 1967. Reported in Herman F. J. Wenzl, The Chemical Technology of Wood. New York: Academic Press, 1970.

Chapter 2

THE PRESENT USE OF WOOD
AS A FUEL

I. INTRODUCTION

By 1960, wood had fallen into near total disuse in this
country, succumbing to competition from the more concentrated
fossil fuels. The 16 years 1960–1976 marked a reversal of that
trend. This reversal resulted from a combination of factors:
the passage of environmental laws, the rapid rise in the costs of
energy, and the appearance of absolute limits to oil and natural
gas availability. The latter two factors, influential in the
U.S. use of wood energy, have played an even more significant
role in the development of energy programs by developing countries. Because of this trend reversal, it is important to define
the amount of wood presently used for energy purposes in the U.S.
From that point, three analyses can proceed: an evaluation of
trends in fuel wood utilization, a comparative assessment of
wood vis-a-vis other fuels, and a comparison of U.S. levels of
fuel wood utilization to consumption levels in other nations.
The purpose of using such data is to determine which historical
trends are being modified and which are being reinforced by this
special case of history – the present.

In the broad sweep of events in the 1960s and 1970s, the
public pushed for a myriad of environmental legislation including the Solid Waste Disposal Act (1965), the Clean Air Act (1967),
the Clean Air Act Amendments (1970), the Clean Water Act (1972),

and a variety of related State and Federal legislation; domestic oil and natural gas production peaked and began to decline; the Arab oil embargo and the quadrupling of international oil prices occurred; and an awareness developed that the nuclear power industry was resource limited and therefore unable to meet its widely heralded expectations. This swirl of environmental and energy-related events provides a backdrop for the resurgence of wood as a fuel source.

II.   UTILIZATION OF WOOD FUELS IN 1976

Because wood fuel consumption statistics have not been col- lected officially since 1950, only rough estimates are available for such years as 1960 and 1970. From that point forward, more data are available. It is known that in 1971, 800,000 homes were heated by wood [1]. Such consumption can be estimated at 0.2×10^{15} Btu. It is also known that in 1971 the pulp and paper industry obtained 0.79×10^{15} Btu by burning wood waste materials [2]. Other industries also consumed modest amounts of wood fuels. At the beginning of this decade, wood was supplying the economy with approximately 1.0×10^{15} Btu of energy [3].

In the absence of official data, the author prepared a detailed estimate of combustible renewable resource utilization in 1976 for the Federal Energy Administration [4]. The results of that investigation are summarized and refined by additional data here, as an introduction to the analysis of current trends. These results are subdivided into wood fuel consumption by the following user communities: the forest products industries, other industries, and residential users.

A.   *The Forest Products Industries*

The forest products industries of the U.S. consumed the vast majority of wood-based fuels in 1976. The pulp and paper industry is the dominant single force in this user community,

consuming nearly 1 quad in the forms of hogged fuel, bark, and
spent pulping liquor [2].   Table I presents wood fuels consumption by this industry in 1976 and shows the contribution of wood
fuels to the total energy budget of the pulp and paper industry.
This energy self-sufficiency in the pulp and paper industry is
distributed unevenly among geographic areas.   The pulp and paper

TABLE I

Fuels Consumed in the Pulp and Paper Industry, 1976[a]

Fuel	Amount (in 10^{12} Btu)	Total (%)
Forest fuels	981.6	44.8
Spent liquor	801.6	36.6
Hogged fuel	82.5	3.8
Bark	97.5	4.4
Fossil fuels	1085.4	49.5
Oil	539.6	24.6
Natural gas	330.5	15.1
Coal	213.4	9.7
Propane	1.9	0.1
Electricity	117.9	5.4
Purchased	107.2	4.9
Self-generated (Hydro)[b]	10.7	0.5
Other	27.6	1.3
Energy sold[c]	(19.4)	(0.9)
Total	2193.1	100.1

[a]Based on the first six months of operation. Data from
Duke and Fudali [2].

[b]Does not include self-generated by cogeneration systems
consuming other fuels.

[c]Represents minimum sales of electricity generated in
excess of in-plant needs.

TABLE II

Use of Residues as Fuel in the Pulp and Paper Industry as a Percentage of Total Energy Consumption (by Region) in 1976[a]

Residue type	Region						
	New England	Middle Atlantic	North Central	South Atlantic	South Central	Mountain & Pacific	National average
Wood chips	2.3	–	0.9	3.0	3.3	9.0	3.7
Bark	3.9	3.0	1.9	6.3	5.9	0.3	4.4
Spent Liquor	23.2	15.3	12.9	43.2	41.2	42.9	36.2
Total	29.4	18.3	15.7	52.5	50.4	52.2	44.3

[a]Data from Duke and Fudali [2].

industry in regions with a preponderance of large, integrated
mills has achieved over 50% energy self-sufficiency. Such
regional trends are presented in Table II.

Table III presents wood fuels consumption among all forest
industries. It shows that, while the pulp and paper industry
consumes far and away the highest volume of wood fuels, there are
similar rates of energy self-sufficiency among the lumber, plywood, and pulp and paper industries. The reason for this dependence stems from the source of these fuels. Bark, sawdust, spent
pulping liquor, and to a large extent hogged fuel are unwanted
residuals of the primary manufacturing processes. These residues
can either be discarded (e.g., in landfills) or combusted to
provide energy. In the case of spent pulping liquor, which contains the energy rich portion of wood (lignin) and valuable pulping chemicals (e.g., sodium), energy recovery is essential to
chemical recovery. Further, discarding the lignin would mean
purchasing an equivalent amount of fossil fuel from outside
sources. That would be expensive indeed for the pulp and paper
industry, already the fourth largest energy consumer in the
U.S. [5].

TABLE III

Wood Fuels Consumption in the Forest Products Industry, 1976[a]

Industry	Energy supplied by wood fuels (in 10^{12} Btu)	Total energy consumed (in 10^{12} Btu)	Wood based energy, % of total fuel consumed
Lumber	35	118	29.7
Plywood	35	70	50.0
Pulp and paper	982	2193	44.8

[a]Source: U.S. Forest Service for 1974 [6] and Duke and
Fudali [2].

B.   Other Industrial Users of Wood Fuels

While the forest products industries consume 1.05×10^{15} Btu
(1.05 quads) of wood based fuels, they are not alone in the consumption of these energy materials. Downstream wood products
manufacturers (e.g., furniture mills), ferroalloy producers, and
a host of other firms also use wood for energy purposes. For
estimating purposes, these groups have been divided into metal-
lurgical firms and all other organizations.

Refiners of ferronickel, ferrosilicon, and copper use varying
amounts and forms of wood in their production processes. Wood
wastes are used most extensively in ferronickel production. The
Riddle Mountain, Oregon, operation of Hanna Mining Co. supplies
10% of U.S. ferronickel requirements. That operation uses the
Ugine process developed by the U.S. Bureau of Mines [7], employing wood chips and sawdust as a heat source and as a reductant.
The nickeliferous ore is dried from 21% to 3–5% water in chip-
fired rotary driers. Sawdust is used as a prereductant in the
calcining step. Then chips are used to reduce ferrosilicon,
since ferrosilicon is the reductant for ferronickel [8].

The 18 operating ferrosilicon plants in the U.S. also use
wood chips as a carbon source. To obtain data on the 1976
consumption of hogged fuel by ferroalloy producers, the producers
of ferrosilicon and ferronickel were surveyed by the author in
December, 1976. Table IV presents the results of that questionnaire survey, which covered production at all ferrosilicon and
ferronickel plants in the U.S. The 100% response resulted in a
0.012×10^{15} Btu annual consumption estimate.

Two copper smelters also utilize wood, employing the ancient
poling process, handed down since at least the days of Agricola
in the fourteenth century, to reduce the oxygen content of copper
from 0.9 to 0.2%. While most copper smelting and refining
operations now use natural gas to accomplish deoxidation,
the White Pine copper smelter in upper Michigan and

TABLE IV

Use of Hogged Fuel in Ferroalloy Production 1976[a]

Firms classification (by tons of wood chips used)	Number of firms	Total wood chip fuel consumption (in 1 × 10⁹ Btu)
0 < 1,000	4	17
1,000 < 10,000	4	362
10,000 < 25,000	3	847
25,000 < 50,000	3	1,634
50,000 < 100,000	2	1,836
> 100,000	3	6,970
Total responses	19	11,666

[a] Data from Tillman [9].

ASARCO-Takoma, Washington smelter still uses wood poles. At current rates of production, some 300×10^9 Btu of wood are used in the refining of this red metal. Total renewable resource utilization in metals refining for 1976 can therefore be estimated at 0.012×10^{15} Btu.

The use of wood as a boiler fuel in all other industries has been calculated from boiler sales data supplied by American Fyr-Feeder Engineers. A survey of 172 installations of American Fyr-Feeder wood-burning boilers indicates that 78.5% are located in forest products manufacturing concerns, 16.3% were installed in furniture and millwork plants, and 5.2% were located in such other places as the U.S. Public Health Service in Atlanta, Georgia. An examination of the boilers sold shows that ∿90% of the capacity was sold to the forest products industry and that ∿10% was sold to downstream or nonwood manufacturing firms. Such data suggest that downstream and nonwood industries consume

about 7% of the amount of total wood fuels utilized, or 0.1
× 10^{15} Btu.

C.   Residential Fuel Wood Utilization

Estimates for 1972, published in 1973, place residential fuel
wood consumption at 0.3×10^{15} Btu/yr [10]. Since that time the
sale of residential wood-fired equipment and cordwood has
increased dramatically [11]. Cordwood in the Northeast has sold
for an average of \$75/cord, or \$3.75/10^6 Btu [12]. To estimate
the present consumption of fuel wood, a questionnaire survey of
36 wood-burning equipment manufacturers was conducted. The
sample consisted of the U.S. Forest Products Laboratory's partial
list of companies in the field. Nine firms responded, seven
filling out the questionnaire and two providing comments only.
Table V presents seven responses. Of these sales, the companies
estimated that 66.7% of the equipment was sold for supplementary
heating and cooking, and 17% for primary heating and cooking.
The additional comments were as follows:

(1) Our products were released in August of 1975. Our 1976
sales were up 175% over '75. We are expecting a 400% increase
in '77 sales over '76; and

(2) I am afraid that we cannot fill out your questionnaire,
due to the fact that we have been manufacturing stoves here for
only the last year. During that period we have made and/or
marketed about 3,500 stoves in four different sizes.

It should be noted that wood-fired systems have been rapid
selling items at auctions [11] and that equipment dealers have
enjoyed a sellers' market in New York and Pennsylvania [12].
Allen L. Hammond has placed the total number of modern wood
stoves sold in recent years at about 500,000 [13]. This represents a more than doubling of residential wood-fired systems
capacity since 1971.

Table V

Estimated Annual Increase in Equipment Sales of Residential
Wood-Fired Equipment[a]

Annual increase in sales since 1972 (%)	Number of firms responding to questionnaire
Negative increase	0
0	0
0 < 25	2
25 < 50	2
50 < 75	0
75 < 100	2
100 < 200	0
200 < 300	1
> 300	0
Total	7

[a]Data from Tillman [9].

Based upon the above data, one can estimate a doubling in the
rate of fuel wood utilization in residential applications since
1970, or a 50% increase since 1972. While these data defy rigorous statistical analysis, a total annual consumption rate of
0.4×10^{15} Btu appears reasonable and conservative.

In addition to the sales of wood-fired equipment, it has been
observed that some 720,000 tons of charcoal (85% made from wood)
were produced in 1976. This represents an additional 15×10^{12}
Btu of wood-based fuel used primarily in residential
applications [14].

D. *Aggregate 1976 Wood Fuels Consumption*

Table VI presents the aggregate statistics for wood fuels consumption. In total, some 1.6×10^{15} Btu of energy come from wood. This 1.6 quads represents a significant increase over 1971, when about 1.0×10^{15} Btu of wood fuels were consumed; and it represents a doubling over the 0.8×10^{15} Btu level of 1960.

TABLE VI

Wood Utilization as Fuel for 1976

User group	Wood and wood residue utilization (in 10^{12} Btu)
Pulp and paper	982
Sawmills, plywood mills, and veneer mills	70
Metallurgical industries	12
Other industries	100
Residential	400
Charcoal	15
Total	1579

III. ANALYSIS OF CURRENT U.S. UTILIZATION PATTERNS

Because of this abrupt reversal in wood fuel consumption trends, it is essential to determine the underlying forces thrusting the utilization of this renewable energy resource forward. Further, it is important to place the present use of wood fuel into the total context of the family of fuels. The utilization of wood should be compared to similar rates for the fossil fuels, nuclear and hydroelectric power, and the nascent energy supplies from municipal and industrial waste.

A. *Recent Trends Underlying U.S. Wood Fuel Utilization*

Analysis of recent trends (1967–1976) in wood fuels consumption must rely upon trends in the pulp and paper industry and the sale of boilers to industrial users. These data are well developed, in contrast to information available in residential wood fuel consumption. Further, the industrial sector is the dominant wood fuels consumer.

Trends in the pulp and paper industry have provided much of the impetus for aggregate growth in the consumption of wood fuels. As Table VII shows, wood fuels consumption by pulp and paper producers increased by 0.2×10^{15} Btu between 1971 and 1976. During that same period, reliance on wood fuels increased from 36 to 45%.

That consumption trend line suggests more fundamental forces operating in the forest fuels arena. Those forces can be identified by an analysis of industrial boiler sales. Until 1967 the percentage of the industrial boiler[1] market supplied by wood and spent pulping liquor-fired boilers was declining slowly.

[1]*The definition of an industrial boiler employed by the American Boiler Manufacturers Assn., and used here, is a unit producing at least 25,000 lb of steam per hour installed in a nonutility facility.*

TABLE VII

Wood Fuels Energy as a Percentage of Total Energy in the Pulp and Paper Industry[a]

Year	Wood fuels consumption (in 10^{12} Btu)	Total fuels consumption (in 10^{12} Btu)	Percentage contributed by wood fuels
1971	790.0	2205.6	36
1972	909.3	2195.7	41
1973	831.9	2163.4	38
1974	854.0	2154.0	40
1975	814.7	1895.7	43
1976	981.6 [b]	2193.1	45

[a] *Data from Duke and Fudali [2] and U.S. Forest Service [6].*
[b] *Based on first six months of 1976.*

From that year forward, however, these fuels have continuously increased their share of the industrial boiler market. Table VIII presents the trends, illustrating the decline from 1962 to 1967, and then the rebounding until 1975.

Since 1972, when natural gas production peaked, wood fuels have commanded 10% of the industrial boiler market. This is particularly significant because the forest industries utilize only 5.8% of the energy consumed by U.S. industry [6]. It demonstrates that wood has commanded the attention of manufacturers outside the forest industries.

To determine what industries have begun utilizing wood as a fuel, the author examined the files of American Fyr-Feeder Engineers of Des Plaines, Illinois. All sales and proposals made from October 1973 through 1977 were categorized by industry type and boiler size. The period selected was the post-Arab oil embargo time frame. It was recognized that selecting such a time period introduces an inconsistency of time frames between these

TABLE VIII

The Sale of Wood Fuels Based Industrial Boilers as a Percentage of Total Industrial Boiler Sales[a]

	Fuel		
Year	Wood	Spent liquor	Total
1962	1.8	2.5	4.3
1963	1.4	6.7	8.1
1964	1.4	4.8	6.2
1965	0.7	6.6	7.3
1966	0.1	5.9	6.0
1967	0.6	1.2	1.8
1968	2.1	3.1	5.2
1969	2.9	4.6	7.5
1970	2.5	5.7	8.2
1971	2.5	5.5	8.0
1972	2.7	7.7	10.4
1973	5.2	5.0	10.2
1974	4.6	5.7	10.3
1975	5.2	4.4	9.6

[a]*Data from Axtman [15].*

examined data and the ABMA statistics. It was felt, however, that such data would highlight the change in interest among non-forest industry firms.

Assuming that these data are representative of total wood fuel using industry trends, exclusive of the pulp and paper industries, then the largest growth has come in the downstream wood products industries. This is the first logical extension of the market for wood-fired boilers, since these firms also generate their fuel in the form of wood residues. A summary table of units sold shows the contrast between the pre- and

TABLE IX

Sales of Boilers by Industry Type and Time Period

| | Industry | | | |
Time period	Forest industries	Downstream industries	Nonwood industries	Total
Pre-embargo boiler sales	110	14	6	130
1973-1977 boiler sales	25	14	3	42
Total	135	28	9	172

post-embargo American Fyr-Feeder Engineers markets. Table IX
reinforces the conclusion that the downstream wood products firms
have experienced the most rapid growth in the use of this fuel.
It should be noted that, in the modern market, all categories of
industries have experienced dramatic growth.

The significance of the influence of time period on the
distribution of boiler sales was analyzed by employing the chi
square (x^2) contingency test. The downstream and nonwood industries columns were combined in order to provide ample numbers of
boilers in each table cell. The x^2 value resulting from this
test was 11.84. The tabular x^2 value at one degree of freedom,
with $\alpha = 0.01$, was 6.635. Thus one can, with certainty, easily
conclude that the recent dramatic increase in wood fuel utilization by downstream and nonwood firms is significantly related to
recent energy events.

An analysis of sales proposals demonstrates that the increase
in wood fuel utilization by downstream and nonwood firms is
continuing. For the period 1973-1977, all categories showed
absolute gains but the nonforest industries showed the most

spectacular gains.   By 1977, downstream manufacturers had become
AFF's premium market.   These trends are shown in Table X.   It
should be noted that, during this period, AFF was not heavily
involved in the pulp and paper industry.   It should also be noted
that a four-year trend in proposals is not substantial enough
evidence for radically altering projections.   At the same time,
this trend toward a broader wood fuel market will apparently
continue.   Proposals show even stronger movement to nonforest
industries than recent unit sales.   Such trends are highlighted
in Table XI.   That pulp and paper is underrepresented in the
modern and potential market data does not diminish that conclusion concerning broader markets for wood in the future.

It can be concluded then that wood fuels in general have
made a strong comeback, particularly since 1972 and the subsequent oil embargo of 1973.   Further, a highly significant shift
has occurred in the market as more wood products manufacturers
such as furniture companies have taken advantage of this energy
source.   That proposals to downstream and nonwood products companies are similar to but somewhat stronger than recent sales
trends suggests that these downstream wood companies and nonwood companies will participate increasingly in the use of wood
fuels during the coming decades.

Why has the use of wood fuels rebounded so strongly?   What
forces have driven this resurgence from less than a quad to 1.6
quads?   These questions are particularly significant in light of
the fact that a wood-fired boiler generally costs $33/lb of
steam/hour of capacity, while an oil- or gas-fired boiler costs
$5/lb of steam/hour [16].   Of those firms seeking proposals from
American Fyr-Feeder Engineers since the embargo, 26 (or 14%)
supplied reasons in their correspondence.   Of these 26, 17 (65%)
cited waste disposal or environmental reasons while 9 (35%)
sought wood due to the increasing cost and scarcity of oil and
natural gas.   This suggests that the synergistic forces that
caused the Ford Motor Co. to install its pyrolysis plant in 1924

TABLE X

Proposals Made by American Fyr-Feeder Engineers Categorized by Industry Type and Boiler Capacity

	Year									
	1973[a]		1974		1975		1976		1977	
Industry type	Units proposed	Total cap.[b]	Units proposed	Total cap.[b]	Units proposed	Total cap.[b]	Units proposed	Total cap.[b]	Units proposed	Total cap.[b]
Forest industries[c]	4	110.0	18	334.1	8	187.0	15	283.0	24	485.2
Downstream manufacturers[d]	6	71.0	21	221.0	10	128.5	12	154.5	28	766.9
Nonwood industries	1	7.5	7	125.5	7	78.8	8	94.0	17	204.6

[a] From October to December 1973 only.

[b] Capacity totals expressed in 10^6 Btu/hour.

[c] Includes significant lumber and plywood but little pulp and paper.

[d] Downstream industries include furniture plants, mobile home manufacturers, and millwork plants.

TABLE XI

Market Distribution by Boiler Sales and Proposals (%) by
Boiler Units

Industry type	Traditional market[a]	Modern market[b]	Near-term potential market[c]
Forest products	84.6	59.5	37.1
Downstream wood manufacturers	10.8	33.3	41.4
Nonwood products companies	4.6	7.2	21.5
Total	100.0	100.0	100.0

[a]Pre-1973 oil embargo sales.
[b]Post-1973 oil embargo sales.
[c]Post-embargo proposals.

and created the entire sawdust burner business again have
emerged. National data can be used to demonstrate the significance of these two forces. The environmental regulation
influence can be seen by correlating the rise in the use of fuel
with the passage of environmental laws. This correlation
appears in Fig. 1. The impetus for the resurgence coincides
with the passage of the Clean Air Act. Two plateaus then appear,
coincident with the major amendments to the Clean Air Act and the
passage of the Clean Water Act. Those plateaus represent waste
disposal and air emission control cost increases that make
energy recovery more economical, and hence increasingly
practiced.

This influence is further suggested by the economic cost of
environmental protection in the pulp and paper industry.
Table XII presents those costs, both in $/ton and as a percentage
of product prices, for 1970 and 1975 [17]. Table XII supports

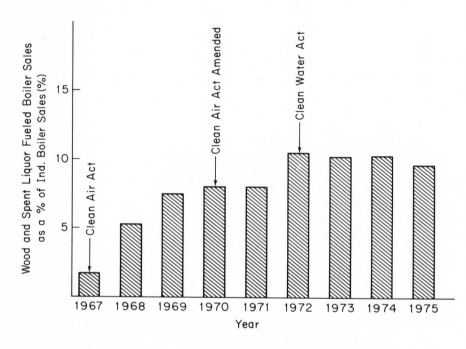

FIGURE 1.   *Boiler sales vs. environmental laws.*

the statements of large wood-fueled boiler manufacturers.   Both
Combustion Engineering and Foster-Wheeler, large wood-fueled
boiler manufacturers, consider energy recovery the most economic
form of waste disposal and cite this as the major factor in the
increasing use of wood as a fuel [18].

Energy price and availability, particularly for oil and gas,
may have also played a modest role in the resurgence of this
fuel.   This is suggested by the American Fyr-Feeder Engineers
correspondence, and by the growth in the use of wood as a fuel
among nonwood product manufacturers.   One can plot the rise in

TABLE XII

The Cost of Pollution Control in the U.S. Pulp and Paper Industry by Type of Product[a]

| Type of product | The cost of pollution control | | | |
| | 1970 | | 1975 | |
	$/ton	Product price (%)	$/ton	Product price (%)
Semichemical pulp	2.55	1.8	13.35	9.7
Sulfite pulp	3.82	2.0	19.85	10.4
Sulfate pulp, paper, and board	2.44	1.3	13.00	6.8
Newsprint	1.00	0.6	4.13	2.3
Other paper and board	1.43	0.6	5.17	2.0

[a]Data from OECD [17].

popularity of wood-fired boilers as the dependent variable, using domestic oil price (a proxy for energy prices) as the independent variable. This yields a regression formula of $y = 0.78x + 4.2$ and a coefficient of correlation $r = 0.62$. That r value is less than significant, even at the 0.25% level. Thus, if a correlation between energy price and wood-fired boiler popularity does exist, it is not a strong one. The American Fyr-Feeder Engineers data provided in Table XI suggest that price and/or availability is more of a future concern than a past one.

In conlusion then, several trends now exist. The use of wood fuels is increasing, and the pulp and paper industry is responsible for much of that increase. The market for such fuels is expanding, particularly as furniture plants and other down-stream wood products manufacturers become involved in the use of wood fuels. The underlying forces behind this use of wood fuel include the costs of waste disposal and pollution control. Energy cost plays only a very modest role in this resurgence of wood.

B.   A Comparison Between the Use of Wood and Other Fuels
     in the U.S.

While the recent trends illustrate changes in the user community of wood-based fuels and provide the critical forces determining projected consumption patterns, the use of wood fuels in
comparison to the rest of the family of fuels determines its
position and, to some extent, its role in the energy picture.
Thus it is important to provide an overview of trends in other
fuels.

During the 1970s, domestic production of oil and natural gas
peaked and began to decline, while coal began a modest comeback
and wastes such as municipal and general industrial refuse began
to be used as fuels. Nuclear power made substantial gains while
hydroelectric power did not increase its contribution to the
economy. It became painfully obvious that imported oil offered
an insecure solution to the problem. It became equally obvious
to energy observers that the long-term solution lay in using a
broad diversity of fuels more extensively, placing less reliance
on a single fuel. Over dependence existed for oil in the 1960s,
coal in the 1910s, or wood in the 1850s. The lesson of diversity
was vital to a society used to simple solutions, but it was one
that the economy had been preparing for. Where there were four
fuels in 1850 - water, wind, wood, and coal - there were 11 in
1976: oil, natural gas, coal, hydroelectric power, nuclear
power, wood-based fuel, urban wastes, agricultural waste, geothermal steam and brines, and solar energy. All of these had
found some application in industry, and some in residential
applications as well. Consumption patterns of these fuels
varied, in some cases by several orders of magnitude as is shown
in Table XIII. Further, growth patterns varied widely, as
Table XIII also demonstrates.

An analysis of these data provides a basis for making some
statements concerning the position of wood fuels in the total

TABLE XIII

Use of Energy in the U.S. by Source, 1960-1976[a]   (in 10^{15} Btu)

Fuel	Year					
	1960	1965	1970	1972	1974	1976
Petroleum						
Domestic[b]	15.6	15.9	20.4	23.7	22.2	20.4
Imported	3.8	5.5	7.0	10.1	12.9	14.9
Natural gas	12.7	16.1	22.0	23.0	22.3	19.9
Coal	10.1	11.9	12.7	12.4	13.0	13.5
Hydro	1.7	2.1	2.7	2.9	2.9	2.9
Nuclear	Negl.	Negl.	0.2	0.6	1.2	1.8
Wood	0.8	0.6	1.0	-	-	1.6
Urban waste	-	-	Negl.	0.05	0.1	0.15
Agricultural waste	-	-	-	-	-	0.03
Geothermal	-	-	0.01	-	-	0.01
Solar	-	-	-	-	-	0.01
Total	44.7+	52.1+	66.0+	73.7+	74.6+	75.1

[a]Data from Hottel and Howard [19], Enzer et al. [20], U.S. Bureau of Mines [21], ERDA [22], and Tillman [23].
[b]Includes natural gas liquids.

family of fuels. Two determinations are necessary: to what extent wood is a growth energy source, and to what extent the combustion of wood is primarily a supplemental energy source as opposed to being primarily a waste disposal solution. Table XIV provides a distribution of fuels by contribution to the economy.

The period 1970-1975 witnessed absolute gains by coal, hydro, nuclear power, and wood. The gains by all other minor fuels, when combined, were modest indeed. Rank ordering of absolute growth places nuclear power in first place (other than imports)

TABLE XIV

Contribution of Selected Fuels to the U.S. Economy (%)

Fuel	Year			
	1960	1965	1970	1975
Petroleum	43.5	41.1	41.5	46.9
Natural gas	28.5	30.9	33.3	26.4
Coal	22.6	22.8	19.2	18.0
Hydro	3.8	4.0	4.1	3.9
Nuclear	Negl.	Negl.	0.3	2.4
Wood	1.6	1.2	1.5	2.1
All others	Negl.	Negl.	Negl.	0.3
Total	100.0	100.0	100.0	100.0

and wood in third. On a percentage contribution basis, only
nuclear power and wood, plus the very minor fuels, increased
their contribution to the U.S. economy. This suggests that,
indeed, wood is a growth energy source if not a primary one.
Fig. 2 offers more supporting data for the contention that wood
is a significant if supplementary fuel among the family of
energy sources. It shows that wood-based fuels have kept pace
with coal in the industrial boiler market during the 1970s [24].

If wood has shown modest growth, how may it be classified
among the family of fuels used in the U.S.? What position does
it occupy? That question can be answered here from a consumption
point of view. In later chapters it will be addressed from a
technical-economic and a resource point of view. To position
the wood fuels, three general classifications are used: primary
fuels, special purpose and/or supplementary fuels, and emerging
as waste disposal fuels. The relative role of each energy form
is shown in Fig. 3.

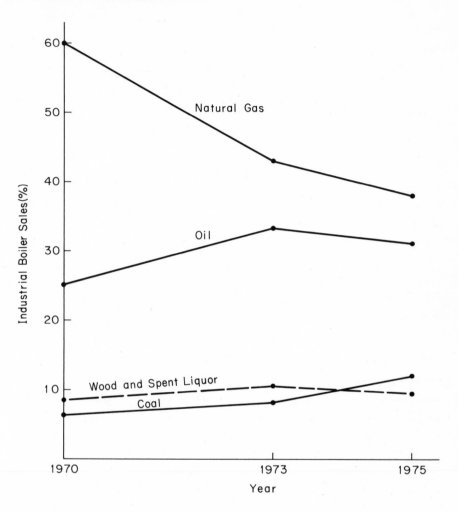

FIGURE 2. Relative position of fuels by industrial boiler sales.

The logarithmic scale is used in Fig. 3 for dramatic purposes only. It highlights the natural segregation of fuels into
classes while permitting the minor fuels to appear on the scale.
The assumption behind the lines of demarcation is that if a fuel
is contributing less than 1×10^{15} Btu the loss of it will have
no appreciable impact on the economy, any sector of the economy
or any geographic region; if a fuel is contributing between

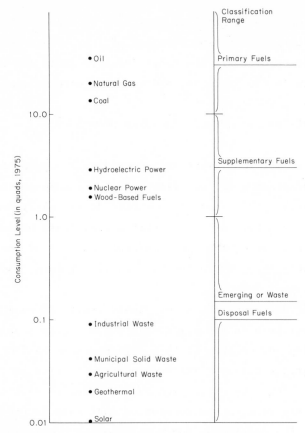

FIGURE 3.   Consumption level (in quads).

1.0×10^{15} and 10.0×10^{15} Btu and it is removed, serious damage
will occur to one or more sectors of the economy or at least one
geographic region; and if a fuel is contributing more than
10×10^{15} Btu, its loss will be felt throughout the nation.

This classification of fuels clearly established wood as a
supplementary fuel source. Its contribution is over 50% of that
made by hydroelectric power and nearly equal to that made by
nuclear power. Its contribution, in fact, represents 67% of the
designed delivery capacity of the Alaskan pipeline [25]. Its
loss would be a crippling if not killing blow to the forest
products industry. This observation is reinforced by the

statements made to Energy User News by a spokesman for the
Chesapeake Corp. That paper company official contended that
without wood-based fuels the paper industry could not compete
economically in the packaging and wrapping materials market [18].

IV. THE PRESENT USE OF WOOD IN OTHER COUNTRIES

Within recent years wood has emerged as a growing fuel in the
U.S. and has assumed the position of being a supplementary energy
source. Despite this impressive record domestically, wood and
wood-based fuels have made more substantial contributions in
other nations. Since those data address aspects of the potential
role that wood can play in the U.S. energy picture, they merit
attention here.

Table XV documents the slow, steady growth of wood harvested
for fuel elsewhere in the world. It shows use by continent
and, in doing so, points out that Asia now uses half of the fuel
wood harvested annually. The continents of Africa and Latin
America hold down the second and third ranks, respectively.

These data lead to the conclusion that wood is far more significant in the developing countries than in the developed
nations. Such conclusions are demonstrated in Table XVI. That
table shows that wood harvested for energy purposes supplies
almost 9% of the energy consumed by developing nations while it
supplies <1% of the energy required by developed economies. The
world average is 3%.

As Tables XV and XVI note, wood residues from manufacturing
processes including spent pulping liquor are not included in the
United Nations data. It is useful then to examine in a cursory
fashion the total contribution of wood in forest based industrial
and industrializing economies. It may be observed that wood,
which supplies 2% of U.S. energy requirements, provides 8% of
Sweden's energy budget, 15% of Finland's energy budget, and

TABLE XV

World Consumption of Fuel Wood, 1971-1975[a,b] *(in 10^{15} Btu)*

	1971	1972	1973	1974	1975
Africa	1.9	2.0	2.0	2.1	2.1
Asia	4.0	4.0	4.1	4.4	4.4
Latin America	1.3	1.3	1.3	1.2	1.2
Europe (including USSR)	1.1	1.1	1.1	0.9	0.9
Oceania	0.1	0.1	0.1	0.1	0.1

[a]*Data from UN 26 .*

[b]*Does not include wastes, hogged fuel, or spent pulping liquor. The exclusion of those data necessarily understates the totals for Europe.*

27% of Brazil's energy expenditures [16]. Brazil has the highest dependency upon wood in its economy.

In Brazil, fossil fuels supply 51.9% of the total energy required by the economy. Oil supplies 48.4%; coal, 3.2%; and natural gas, 0.3%. Renewable or inexhaustible sources supply 48.1% of that nation's needs with wood and bagasse contributing 27.4% and hydro contributing 20.7% of that nation's energy needs [27].

Two primary industries use wood fuels in Brazil: pulp and paper, and steel. The pulp and paper industry produces 1.83×10^6 tons (1.66×10^6 tonnes) or 1.3% of total world production. This industry is fueled by its own residues. The steel industry uses charcoal to reduce 29% of its iron ore into pig iron. Some 3 million tons of pig iron, out of a total national production of 10 million tons, are produced in this

TABLE XVI

Fuelwood as a Percentage of Total energy Supply[a]   (in 10^{15} Btu)

Nations	Total energy consumption			Fuel wood consumption			Fuel wood as percentage of total energy supply		
	1971	1973	1975	1971	1973	1975	1971	1973	1975
Developed[b,c]	178.9	190.8	199.1	0.5	0.4	0.4	0.3	0.2	0.2
Developing	85.3	101.3	94.8	8.0	8.3	8.4	9.4	8.2	8.9
World	265.1	292.6	294.8	8.5	8.7	8.8	3.2	3.0	3.0

[a]Data from Axtman [24].

[b]This data does not include waste wood or spent liquor. The absence of data on waste wood and spent liquor artificially reduces this number, hence the percentage contribution of wood as an energy source to the economies of developed nations.

[c]Includes centrally planned economies.

manner [28]. This success in steel production has caused Japan
to investigate the potential for using forest energy plantations
and charcoal to fuel its steel industry [28].

Brazil uses other renewable resource fuels as well. Its
motor vehicle population is fueled by a blend of 85% gasoline:
15% ethanol. The ethanol comes primarily from the sugar cane
industry, with only modest amounts being produced from wood and
wood residues [27].

Other nations have also promoted alternatives biomass fuels.
After the development of the Gobar biogas plant in 1939, Asia
moved significantly in this direction. Today China has 500,000
such plants, India has 100,000, and South Korea has 50,000 [29].
These systems use manure and crop residues as a fuel. Taiwan had
been an early user of this technology, particularly during the
Japanese occupation during World War II [30]. After a period of
disuse, biogas has returned to favor there, and 7500 units have
been installed [31]. Thus in Asia where 12% of the energy comes
from fuel wood, renewable resources in toto play as vital a role
as coal does in the U.S. Throughout the rest of the world in
general, renewable resources are more significant for energy
purposes than they are in North America.

V.   IMPLICATIONS FOR THE FUTURE OF WOOD FUELS IN THE U.S.

What salient forces have emerged, both within and outside the
U.S. in recent years, to promote or constrain the use of wood-
based fuels for the rest of this century? The trends and forces
identified in the U.S. and international segments of this chapter can be categorized into the following types: forces in U.S.
in wood fuels consumption as they relate to forces in total U.S.
energy consumption, and forces in total wood fuels consumption.

Certainly wood fuels can again be considered growth fuels.
Their increasing contribution to the U.S. economy in absolute
and relative terms demonstrates this growth. Their expanding

markets in both industrial and residential settings also prove
the point. At the same time, however, wood fuels rely upon
synergistic forces to be economical. The combination of environmental protection and energy cost is the most potent synergistic
combination extant.

While wood has been increasing its contribution, the U.S.
economy has been making more use of a wider range of fuels. At
the same time it has been placing less and less reliance on its
primary fuels. In 1974, the peak year of domination by oil,
petroleum supplied the economy 47.9% of its fuels; and petroleum
and natural gas combined to supply 77% of the nation's energy
needs. This contrasts with 1910, when coal supplied 76.8% of the
nation's energy and coal plus wood supplied 87.4%. In 1850 and
the years before that time, wood supplied over 90% of the
nation's energy requirement and the combination of wood and coal
provided virtually all of the nation's fuel [20,32]. That the
domination by primary fuels remains perhaps excessive does not
deny the fact that more fuels are being used and that these fuels
are increasing their absolute and relative contribution.

Wood is one such resource that, because of the magnitude of
its contribution, is economically significant as a supplementary
fuel. Industrial boiler sales for wood-based fuels have, in
fact, kept pace with those for coal. Thus, despite the need for
an environment-energy synergy, wood fuel utilization cannot be
considered a waste disposal option of little energy importance.

While the resurgence of wood fuels in the U.S. is impressive,
these fuels remain far more significant in other nations, including some industrial economies. It would be folly to suggest
that wood will ever be as significant in the U.S. as it is
in Brazil, but these international data strongly suggest that
forest fuels can significantly increase their contribution to
the U.S. economy over present levels.

REFERENCES

1. A. A. Putnam, E. L. Kropp, and R. E. Barrett, Evaluation of
    National Boiler Inventory. Prepared for Industrial
    Environmental Research Laboratory. Columbus, Ohio:
    Battelle Columbus Laboratories, October, 1975.

2. J. M. Duke and M. J. Fudali, Report on the Pulp and Paper
    Industry's Energy Savings and Changing Fuel Mix. New York:
    American Paper Institute, September, 1976.

3. Renewable Resources for Industrial Materials. Report of the
    Committee on Renewable Resources for Industrial Materials.
    Washington, D.C.: Nat. Acad. Sci., 1976.

4. David A. Tillman, The Contribution of Non-Fossil Organic
    Materials to U.S. Energy Supply. Washington, D.C.:
    Materials Associates, Inc., Feb. 15, 1977 (under FEA
    Contract P-03-77-4426-0).

5. John G. Meyers, et al., Energy Consumption in Manufacturing
    (report to the Energy Policy Project of the Ford Foundation).
    Cambridge, Massachusetts: Ballinger, 1974.

6. U.S. Forest Service, The Feasibility of Utilizing Forest
    Residues for Energy and Chemicals (report to the National
    Science Foundation and Federal Energy Administration).
    Washington, D.C.: Forest Service, USDA, March, 1976.

7. L. H. Banning and W. E. Anable, Preliminary Electric
    Smelting Research on Philippine Nickeliferous Ores, Report
    of Investigations 5129. Washington, D.C.: U.S. Dept.
    of the Interior, Bureau of Mines, May, 1955.

8. The Hanna Nickel Operation. Riddle, Oregon: The Hanna
    Mining Co., June 1, 1970.

9. David A. Tillman, Uncounted energy: Renewable organic
    resources, in Fuels and Energy from Renewable Resources
    (D. A. Tillman, K. V. Sarkanen, and L. L. Anderson, eds.).
    New York: Academic Press, 1977.

10. Ed Cliff, Timber, the Renewable Resource. Washington, D.C.: National Commission on Materials Policy, 1973.

11. Charles J. Jordan and Jessie S. Cole, The shape of things to come, Yankee, Jan. 1974.

12. Mary Ellen Perry, Warming up to those old wood stoves, The Washington Star, Feb. 5, 1977.

13. Allen L. Hammond, Photosynthetic solar energy: Rediscovering biomass fuels, Science, Aug. 19, 1977.

14. Charcoal Briquet Institute, Interview with Arthur Seeds, Dec. 28, 1976.

15. William Axtman, American Boiler Manufacturers Assn., personal interview, Nov. 2, 1976.

16. Thomas B. Reed, When the oil runs out, in Capturing the Sun Through Bioconversion, Proceedings. Washington, D.C.: Council on Solar Biofuels, March 10-12, 1976.

17. Pollution by the Pulp and Paper Industry: Present Situation and Trends. Paris: Organization for Economic Cooperation and Development, 1973.

18. Alan Dell, Waste-fired boiler firms gird for booming market, Energy User News, Mar. 14, 1977.

19. H. C. Hottel and J. B. Howard, New Energy Technology - Some Facts and Assessments. Cambridge, Massachusetts: MIT Press, 1971.

20. Herman Enzer, Walter Dupree, and Stanley Miller, Energy Perspectives, Vol. I. Washington, D.C.: U.S. Dept. of the Interior, Feb. 1975.

21. Commodity Data Summaries 1977. Washington, D.C.: U.S. Bureau of Mines, Dept. of the Interior, 1977.

22. A National Plan for Energy Research, Development and Demonstration: Creating Energy Choices for the Future, 1976, Vol. 1: The Plan. Washington, D.C.: Energy Research and Development Administration, Apr. 1976.

23. David A. Tillman, Combustible renewable resources, Chemtech, Oct. 1977.

24. W. H. Axtman, <u>Shift in Boiler Fuel Usage Patterns</u>.
     Washington, D.C.:   American Boiler Manufacturers Assn.,
     1977.

25. Richard D. James, A controversy looms over the price to
     place on Alaskan crude oil, <u>Wall Street Journal</u>, Apr. 15,
     1977.

26. <u>World Energy Supplies 1971-1975</u>. New York: Dept. of
     Economic and Social Affairs, United Nations (Statistical
     Papers Ser. J, No. 20), 1977.

27. Rosely Maria Viegas Assumpcao, presentation before <u>Symp.</u>,
     <u>Fuels and Energy from Renewable Resources</u>, American
     Chemical Society, Aug. 31, 1977, Chicago, Illinois.

28. Tree plantations eyed for charcoal, <u>Energy User News</u>,
     June 27, 1977.

29. Russell W. Peterson, The ecology of bioconversion, in <u>Proc.</u>
     <u>Capturing the Sun through Bioconversion</u>. Washington, D.C.:
     Council on Solar Biofuels, March 10-12, 1976.

30. Chung Po, <i>et al.</i>, Small methane generator for waste disposal,
     in <u>Proc., Managing Livestock Waste: Third Int. Symp. Live-
     stock Wastes</u>. St. Joseph, Michigan: Am. Soc. Agricultural
     Eng., April 21-24, 1975.

31. Chung Po, Production and use of methane from animal waste
     in Taiwan, in <u>Proc. Int. Biomass Energy Conf</u>. Winnipeg,
     Canada: Biomass Energy Inst., 1973.

32. Sam H. Schurr and Bruce C. Netschert, <u>Energy in the
     American Economy, 1850-1975</u>. Baltimore, Maryland: Johns
     Hopkins Univ. Press, 1960.

Chapter 3

THE VALUE OF WOOD
AS A FUEL

I. INTRODUCTION

In considering the future of wood as an energy resource, it
is useful to understand historical and current utilization patterns. Such patterns provide two bases for examining the future.
However, an assessment of the future of wood in the energy arena
depends upon defining its intrinsic value and position within
the family of combustible fuels. Establishing such a definition
or evaluation is all the more important because of claims made
by promoters and detractors of wood fuels. The promoters claim
wood is a premium grade energy source, while detractors consider
it next to useless. The real value lies somewhere between these
claims. Thus a clear and objective positioning is mandated.

The hard reality is that there is no one wood fuel. There
are many wood fuels. The premier wood fuel is, of course, charcoal. It is followed, in descending order (not exhaustive), by
dry softwood material (e.g., pellets, planer shavings), air
dried hardwood, as-received hog fuel, spent liquor where the
energy rich lignin is concentrated, and ultimately as-received
bark. In the fuels listed above, heat content varies from
12,000 Btu/lb (charcoal), to 8800 Btu/lb (pellets), to 3000
Btu/lb (wet bark). Moisture varies from 1.5% (charcoal) to 67%
(bark). Sulfur and ash range from negligible to very

significant as one goes from pellets to spent pulping liquor.
This variety, as represented by the materials listed above, is
hard to overstate. It is within this framework of diversity that
a definition of the position of wood fuels must be made.

In establishing such a definition, it is essential to consider the chemical composition of wood and the polymers that
combine to form wood. It is then necessary to examine the
relationship between the chemical compositions so identified and
the heating value of wood. Following the discussion of heating
value must be an evaluation of the other elements and compounds
contained in this fuel material and how they affect its energy
value. Throughout it is necessary to analyze relationships
between the composition, heating value, and impurities of wood
and the same parameters as they exist in the other combustible
fuels.

In developing the relationships between wood and other combustible fuels, an implicit if not explicit departure is made
from the current convention of considering biomass fuels as
solar energy. This solar energy approach considers photosynthe-
sis as a means of solar conversion. Such an analysis leads to
the conclusion that fossil fuels, like biomass, are solar energy.
It ends up agglomerating biomass, fossil fuels, flat plate sun-
light collection systems, ocean thermal systems, wind, photo-
voltaic cells, and more into one unwieldy energy supply category.

Fossil fuels, however, are normally removed and considered
as a separate class of energy sources. In the approach taken
here biomass fuels, particularly wood, are included with fossil
fuels in that class called combustible fuels. Such a modest
adjustment permits the development of consistent criteria for
fuel value analysis, particularly from a user point of view.

II.   WOOD AS A COMBUSTIBLE FUEL

One can no more consider wood as one fuel than one can discuss all types of coal, analytically, in the same breath. Wood
fuels vary by tree species and wood material (e.g., bark, heartwood, sapwood, needles). While the physical structure (e.g.,
cell walls) is not an important parameter in determining the
energy value of wood materials, the chemical composition is of
critical importance. Wood is a composite of three basic polymers: cellulose $(C_6H_{10}O_5)$, lignin $(C_9H_{10}O_3(OCH_3)_{0.9-1.7})$, and
the hemicelluloses such as xylan $(C_5H_8O_4)$. Added to these
materials are extractives and minerals or ash.

A.   Wood Composition and Heating Value

In general, hardwoods contain about 43% cellulose, 22% lignin, and 35% hemicelluloses (on an extractive free basis) while
softwoods contain about 43% cellulose, 29% lignin, and 28% hemicellulose [1]. The specific composition of seven species of
North American woods, along with their energy contents, is presented in Table I. As species vary in composition, so do parts
of the tree itself. Further, residues such as bark, sawdust,
planer shavings and spent pulping liquor, vary in energy value
and, concomitantly, chemical composition.

The different chemical compositions are responsible for varying heat contents among wood fuels. Holocellulose (cellulose
and hemicellulose) and lignin offer significantly different heats
of combustion: 7527 Btu/lb for holocellulose and 11,479 Btu/lb
for Douglas fir lignin [1]. The extractives also contain high
energy contents, sometimes approaching 15,000 Btu/lb. As
Table I shows, there is some association between the lignin content and the energy value. This association is to be expected.
It supports the general statement that as the lignin and extractives content of wood species rise, so does the higher heating
value of the fuel produced.

TABLE I

Chemical Composition of 10 Species of North American Woods[a,b]

Tree species	Cellulose (%)	Lignin (%)	Hemi- celluloses (%)	Btu/lb
Beech	45.2	22.1	32.7	8455
White birch	44.5	18.9	36.6	8334
Red maple	44.8	24.0	31.2	8400
Eastern white cedar	48.9	30.7	20.4	8400
Eastern hemlock	45.2	32.5	22.3	8885
Jack pine	45.0	28.6	26.4	8930
White spruce	48.5	27.1	21.4	8890

[a]Extractive free basis, dry weight basis.
[b]Sources: [2,3,4,5].

These data suggest the following general formula for determining the approximate heating value of wood on a dry weight ash-free basis:

$$HHV \doteq C \times 7527 + (1 - C) \times 11,479$$

where HHV is the higher heating value in Btu/lb and C the fraction of wood consisting of holocellulose. The formula provides a reasonable approximation based upon the simplifying assumption that lignin provides most of the higher energy values in wood fuel. The absence of data on extractives necessarily prevents the development of a more precise formula; however, that formula associates extractives with the lignin which also has a high energy value. Applying the formula to the seven species in Table I, one obtains a mean heating value of 8559 Btu/lb, as opposed to the mean of 8613 Btu/lb for the literature values. For all species in Table I, the formula provides a mechanism for

predicting *HHV* within ±350 Btu/lb. The average difference
between the observed and predicted value is 164 Btu/lb.

The composition of wood determines both its heat content
and how it releases useful energy. All wood combustion and conversion begins with pyrolysis. In pyrolysis holocellulose principally promotes the release of volatiles while lignin, which
also releases volatiles, primarily promotes char formation [1].
The volatiles produced burn directly in flaming combustion or
provide wood gas. The char oxidizes in glowing combustion, is
used as charcoal, or is gasified. Fig. 1 shows the relationship
between heat content and char yield.

A more traditional approach to combustible fuels evaluation
employs the ultimate analysis of the candidate material. These
analyses may or may not include ash; they may or may not include
moisture content. They are not unrelated to the analyses previously presented (e.g., increasing the relative proportion of
lignin increases the relative proportion of carbon). Ultimate
analysis can be employed to evaluate charcoal fuels as well as
wood materials per se.

Table II presents the ultimate analysis of numerous wood
fuels on a dry weight basis. The Btu/lb values presented are
higher heating values. These data demonstrate generally that
wood is a highly oxygenated fuel with about two-thirds the energy
content of coal. Softwoods generally contain more energy than
hardwoods on a dry weight basis due to higher lignin (hence
carbon) content plus the presence of more resins in the extrac-
tions [9].

The ultimate analysis shown in Table II suggests that the
correspondence between carbon content and higher heating value
is more than a casual relationship. That they march together in
lockstep has been demonstrated conclusively by Shafizadeh [1].
Shafizadeh concludes that, for such solid fuels a mutual can-
cellation minimizes, if not eliminates, the influence of hydrogen and oxygen. For the data presented in Table II, a linear

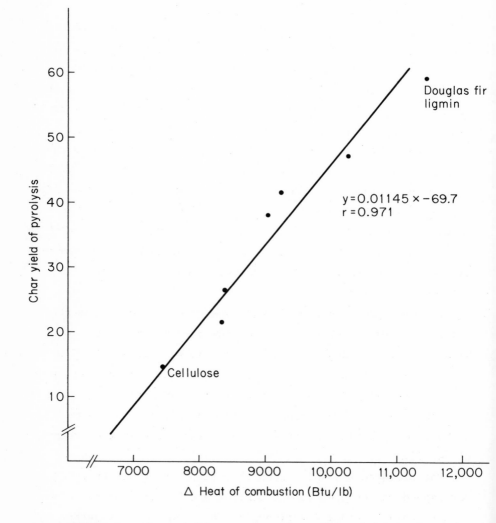

FIGURE 1.   Char yield as a function of total heat of
combustion.

TABLE II

Ultimate Analysis of Selected Forest Fuels[a,b]

	Fuel									
	Charcoal		Softwoods				Hardwoods			
Elemental analysis	Tech-air[c]	Tech-air[d]	Douglas fir	Douglas fir bark	Western hemlock	Red wood	Beech	Hickory	Maple	Poplar
Carbon	75.3	80.3	52.3	56.2	50.4	53.5	51.64	49.67	50.64	51.64
Hydrogen	3.8	3.1	6.3	5.9	5.8	5.9	6.26	6.49	6.02	6.26
Oxygen	15.2	11.3	40.5	36.7	41.4	40.3	41.45	43.11	41.74	41.45
Nitrogen	0.8	0.2	0.1	0.0	0.1	0.1	0.0	0.0	0.25	0.0
Sulfur	0.0	0.0	0.0	Trace	0.1	0.0	0.0	0.0	0.0	0.0
Ash	3.4	3.4	0.8	1.2	2.2	0.2	0.65	0.73	1.35	0.65
Btu/lb	12,094	13,370	9050	9500	8620	9040	8760	8670	8580	8920

[a] Dry weight basis, HHV basis.
[b] Sources: [3,6,7,8].
[c] Sawdust and pine bark pyrolyzed at 750°F (400°C).
[d] Sawdust and pine bark pyrolyzed at 930°F (500°C)

regression equation of $y = 151.91x$ has been developed.   This
equation shows that, for each percentage increase in carbon, the
higher heating value of wood increases by 151.91 Btu/lb.   In
conclusion, then, the higher heating value of wood (O.D. basis)
is in the vicinity of 9000 Btu/lb.   Variations in this value
result from lignin and to a lesser extent extractives content,
or the carbon content of the fuel.

B.   *A Comparison of the Heating Value of Wood to Other*
     Combustible Fuels

The previous discussion presented a general analysis of the
heating value of wood by itself.   In order to make definitive
statements concerning the position of wood within the class of
combustible fuels, however, a comparative evaluation must be
made.   It is here that the importance of reclassifying biomass
with fossil energy into a class, combustible fuels, becomes
important.   It is also in this process that the ultimate analysis
of fuels becomes critical.

Table III presents 15 ultimate analyses of fuels from dried
sewage sludge through Utah bituminous coal.   In higher heating
value (dry basis), they range from 2040 Btu/lb to 14170 Btu/lb.
Ash contents range from 1.0 to 71.4% and oxygen contents range
from 4.9 to 51.2%.   All analyses were obtained from the literature cited.

The data presented in Table III have been plotted in Fig. 2,
a least squares line showing carbon content and higher heating
value.   The general equation describing the line is as follows:

$y = 188.0x - 131.5$

where y is the higher heating value and x the percentage of
carbon.   The coefficient of correlation of this empirically
observed relation is $r = 0.982$.   The coefficient of determination is $r^2 = 0.965$. It can be noted then that the curve derived
from Table II is probably a segment of this larger curve

TABLE III

Ultimate Analysis of Selected Fuels[a]

Fuel material	Ultimate Analysis (dry wt basis)						
	C	H	O	N	S	Ash	Btu/ lb
Utah coal	77.9	6.0	9.9	1.5	0.6	4.1	14,170
Pittsburgh coal #1	75.5	5.0	4.9	1.2	3.1	10.3	13,650
Pittsburgh coal #2	73.3	5.3	10.2	0.7	2.8	7.6	13,097
Wyoming coal	70.0	4.3	20.2	0.7	1.0	13.8	14,410
Douglas fir bark	56.2	5.9	36.7	0.0	0.0	1.2	9,500
Wood	52.0	6.3	40.5	0.1	0.0	1.0	9,000
Pine bark	52.3	5.8	38.8	0.2	0.0	2.9	8,780
Bagasse	47.3	6.1	35.3	0.0	0.0	11.3	9,140
Raw sewage	45.5	6.8	25.8	2.4	0.5	19.0	7,080
Bovine waste	42.7	5.5	31.3	2.4	0.3	17.8	7,380
Rice hulls	38.5	5.7	39.8	0.5	0.0	15.5	6,610
Rice straw	39.2	5.1	35.8	0.6	0.1	19.2	6,540
MSW	33.9	4.6	22.4	0.7	0.4	38.0	5,645
Paper mill sludge	30.9	7.2	51.2	0.5	0.2	10.2	5,350
Sewage sludge	14.2	2.1	10.5	1.1	0.7	71.4	2,040

[a]*Sources:* [7,8,10-13].

describing the influence of carbon on the higher heating value
of solid combustible fuels. The oil value presented in Fig. 2
was not used in the equation. Oil and natural gas vary substantially from solid fuels in that hydrogen plays a significant
role in determining energy value.

Based upon this solid fuels curve, certain statements can be
made concerning the relationship of wood fuels to the total
family of combustible fuels. The premium fuels are those where

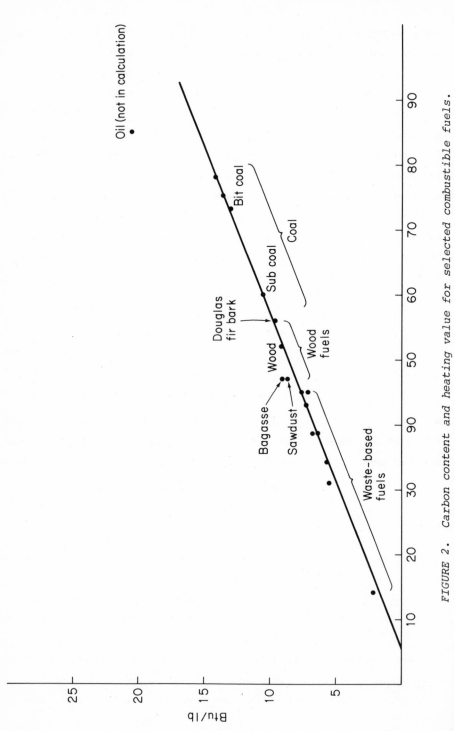

FIGURE 2. Carbon content and heating value for selected combustible fuels.

both hydrogen and carbon contribute significantly to the energy value. This excludes coal and all other fuels on the carbon curve posited in Fig. 2. Wood is the transition fuel between the waste materials (∿5000–∿7500 Btu/lb) and coal (∿10,000–∿14,000 Btu/lb). Fig. 3 depicts such positions. These data suggest that the three categories of combustible fuel employed in Chapter 2 are value as well as consumption oriented. The first category, primary fuels, splits into two subgroups: premium and subpremium. The second category, supplementary fuels, corresponds with the transition category of this discussion. The third category, waste based fuels, is identical in both chapters. For the development of projections, it is important to establish whether the transition category displays a closer proximity to primary fuels or to waste-based fuels. Such refined positioning provides more substance to the categories posited above.

One such affinity measure of this relative energy value is Btu/ft^3. This measure is of more than casual interest for it addresses costs associated with transportation, storage, and materials handling. Table IV presents representative values for fuels on the carbon curve Btu/ft^3. Bagasse and municipal waste are employed as representatives of the waste fuels. Among the wastes now combusted for energy purposes, they are the most frequently used materials other than wood. From Table IV it is clear that wood is the transition material between wastes and fossil fuels. However, there is a closer proximity between wood and the wastes than between wood and coal.[1]

---

[1] *It should be noted that the values for wood and coal presented in Tables III and IV can be anticipated from an investigation of the process of coal formation. While such a consideration is outside the scope of this text, excellent descriptions include the following references [15,16,17]. These papers offer insight into the decomposition of holocellulose and lignin, at different rates, and the subsequent formation of coal.*

TABLE IV

Heating Value/ft^3 for Selected Fuels^a (Dry weight basis)

Fuel	Lb/ft^3	Btu/ft^3
Bituminous coal	52.0	676,000
Charcoal	15.25	198,250
Hogged fuel	18.0	162,000
Bark	24.0	220,000
Bagasse	5.0	45,500
Municipal waste	10.0	56,450

^{a}Source: [14].

III.   OTHER ELEMENTS AND COMPOUNDS

While Btu/ft^3 provides one approach in measuring the affinity of transition fuels to waste or primary fuels, a discussion of the other elements and compounds contained in each fuel provide more conclusive results. The materials considered here are those which either cause pollution or directly impair the heating value of a fuel. These include not only the traditional pollutants considered in discussions of fossil fuels; but also, separately, moisture. Water reduces heating value and can contribute to pollution control problems.

A.   Potential Pollutants Analysis

Traditionally, sulfur and ash are considered the principal impurities in combustible fuels. The sulfur, on combustion, forms SO_2 which is a pollutant in its own right. It also can combine with rain to form dilute sulfurous acid, or can transform, in the atmosphere into other potentially dangerous compounds. The ash results in the release of particulates up the smokestack. These pollutants can be controlled by devices such as stack gas scrubbers, the U.S. Bureau of Mines citrate

process, electrostatic precipitators and baghouse installations.
All such installations, however, reduce the energy efficiency of
a given energy using operation (e.g., a power plant).

The ultimate analyses presented in Table II show wood to be
very low in sulfur and ash. For the eight species presented, the
mean sulfur content is 0.013% (by wgt) and the mean ash content
is 1.12%. These values demonstrate that wood is essentially
pollution free, although wood combustion requires some particulate control measures.

The ultimate analyses presented in Table III show other solid
combustible fuels to be in a less favorable position. Coal, for
example, has sulfur contents ranging from 0.6 to 3.1%. It is
well known that Illinois coal can have 5+% sulfur, creating significant SO_2 control problems. Ash content varies from 4.1 to
13.8% in Table III. Lignite coals from North Dakota and Texas
are even higher in ash content. The waste based fuels are low
in sulfur (mean value from Table III, 0.3%). Ash content is a
serious problem, as all waste fuels have in excess of 10%
inorganic matter. The mean of the values presented in Table III
is 25.3% ash, with municipal waste (38.0% ash) and sewage sludge
(71.4% ash) having the most severe problems.

From the point of view of controlling formation of SO_2 and
prohibiting the release of particulate matter, wood is a more
desirable fuel than any of the other solid fuels. In an era of
environmental consciousness, this advantage is a compelling
attraction for the premium biomass energy source.

B. *Moisture Analysis*

Wood does suffer from the presence of moisture in significant
quantities. Fresh wood may contain upward of 22 to 55% H_2O
(wgt %, total material basis) and at times may contain as much
as 67% moisture (total weight or as-received basis). Moisture,
more than any single variable, segregates the class of wood
fuels into the distinct and separate fuel types identified

in the introduction. The moisture classification successfully
denotes the many variations in wood fuel because the moisture
content significantly influences the net heating value of wood
fuels, the ignition properties, and the efficiency of fuel utilization. The first two issues will be dealt with here since they
are strictly questions of fuel value. Efficiency will be
treated in Chapter 4 in discussions of combustion and conversion
systems.

The influence of moisture on higher heating value can be
calculated by the following formula [9]:

$$NHV/\text{lb} = HHV/\text{lb} - \left[L_w + L_{hv} \right]$$

where NHV is the net heating value, HHV the higher heating value,
L_w the loss in weight of combustible products as water replaces
wood, and L_{hv} the loss due to heat of vaporization required to
remove the water. The above conceptual formula leads to a more
precise general formula which, when related to the previous
formula, appears as follows:

$$NHV = HHV - [0.0114 \; (HHV) \times M]$$

where M is the moisture content, expressed as a percent of total
as-received fuel material. A $\chi^2_{\alpha = 0.01}$ test performed on this
second formula over a sample of as-received wood fuels shows an
extremely close fit between observed and calculated values.
Thus the second formula provides a useful method for calculating
the net heat content of wood fuels.

Fig. 3 graphically depicts the influence of water on the
energy value of as-received wood fuel. As is shown, there is a
practical limit of combustibility, or black-out zone, at 67%
water, 33% wood.

The influence of water on ignition is as serious as its
influence on net energy content. Table V presents time and
temperature points for the ignition of air-dried wood (~12–15%

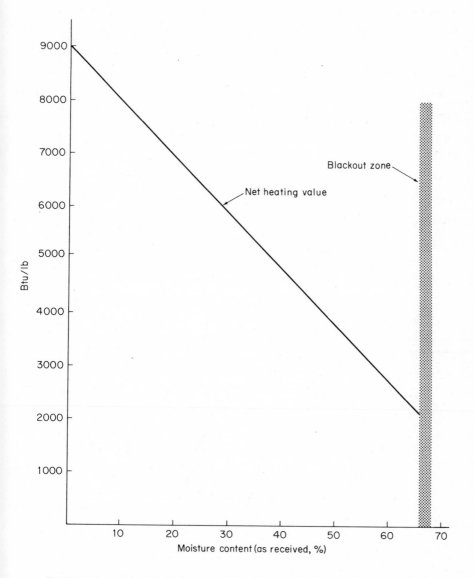

FIGURE 3. The influence of moisture on the heating value of wood.

TABLE V

The Time and Temperature Required for Wood Ignition as a
Function of Moisture Content[a]

Tempera-ture of heating (°F)	Average time before ignition (minutes)					
	Tamarak		Longleaf pine		Hemlock	
	AD	OD	AD	OD	AD	OD
392	–	15	24	12	24	13
437	31	10	18	9	15	7
482	21	6	11	6	10	4
527	14	4	7	3	7	3
572	10	2	5	2	5	2
617	6	1	3	1	3	1
662	3	<1	2	<1	2	<1
707	2	<1	1	<1	1	<1
752	1	<1	<1	<1	<1	<1

[a]Source: [20].

moisture) and oven-dried wood ($\sim$5–8% moisture). These time and
temperature differences represent the energy expenditure required
to evaporate the moisture contained in the wood, and to begin the
process of combustible volatile for motion. Thus the energy,
hence economic, value of the wood is again impaired.

Probably the best explanation of the influence of moisture
on heat release and heat of preignition is provided by Shafizadeh
[19]. Using a variety of analytical techniques including thermal
analysis, thermal evolution analysis, and the employment of a
reaction coulometer, he has demonstrated that for dry cellulose,
the energy required to obtain ignition at $\sim$575°F is $\sim$225 Btu/lb
and the net heat release is $\sim$5070 Btu/lb. For cellulose containing 50% moisture (as-received basis) at $\sim$600°F, the respec-
tive values are $\sim$1450 Btu/lb input to achieve ignition and

∿3700 Btu/lb net heat release. This is grapically depicted in
Fig. 10 of that paper.

Because the influence of water is so significant, it is
essential to determine the average moisture content of as-
received wood fuels. Table VI presents these data for 17 species
on a cordwood basis. The average moisture content is 37.2%, and
the range is from 21.3 to 55.1%. Hardwoods and softwoods fall
into two separate classes, however. Hardwoods contain, on
average, 30.2% moisture (with a range from 21.3% to 39.3%) while
softwoods contain, on average, 46.1% water on a total weight
basis. Thus one can estimate an average net heating value of
6500 Btu/lb for hardwoods and 4000 Btu/lb for softwoods on an as-
received basis. This marks an abrupt reversal from the energy
content on a dry weight basis and, in so doing, demonstrates the
significance of the moisture impurity.

It should be recognized that the values given in Table VI
are averages, probably for mature wood. Moisture content is a
function not only of species, but also of tree age and the
material of the tree in consideration. Younger trees, particularly those in the highest stages of growth, contain far more
moisture than those which are growing slowly or not at all. Further the foliage of a tree (e.g., the leaves, needles, and
branches) is more moisture laden than the bole. Within the bole
the sapwood contains more water than the heartwood. Thus, for
any given energy recovery process, all of these moisture related
variables must be considered when analyzing the fuel feedstock.
The averages of Table VI are useful, however, for illustrating
the relative importance of moisture by species and by wood type
(e.g., hardwoods, softwoods). Further they provide a useful
approximation for comparative purposes.

Moisture content is not inherent in coal, particularly coals
of a higher rank (e.g., Pittsburgh seam bituminous coal). It
can be present in the lignites. The moisture problem is endemic

TABLE VI

Typical Moisture Content of As-Received Wood Fuels[a,b]

Wood	Lbs/ft^3 green	Lbs water/ft^3 green	% water
Ash, white	47	10	21.3
Hickory	65	15	23.1
Beech	54	14	25.9
Elm	53	14	26.4
Oak, white	59	17	28.8
Maple	58	19	32.8
Birch, white	51	18	35.3
Cedar, white	28	10	35.7
Pine, white	39	15	38.5
Oak, red	65	25	38.5
Oak, black	61	24	39.3
Pine, pitch	54	22	40.7
Cyprus	47	22	46.8
Pine, yellow	49	24	49.0
Poplar	49	24	49.0
Fir	52	28	53.8
Hemlock	49	27	55.1
Average	51.8	19.3	37.2

[a] *Source: [21].*

[b] *Cord wood rather than hogged fuel basis. Hogged fuel has a lbs/ft^3 value of ~50% that for cordwood.*

to all biomass fuels where H_2O contents range from 20 to 50% or greater among the municipal waste, crop waste, and feedlot waste categories [7,12]. Thus wood is in a disadvantageous position with respect to coal. Further, it has no particular advantage when compared to the other biomass fuels. This stands in stark contrast to previous analysis of carbon content (dry weight basis) and pollutant content. It perhaps is the dominant factor explaining the proximity of wood to wastes, as opposed to coal, in total energy value.

IV. CONCLUSION: TOTAL COMPARATIVE FUELS DISCUSSION

It is useful, in developing a total comparison among fuels, to recast key ultimate analysis data to include typical moisture content information. This is provided in Table VII. It highlights critical comparisons which must be made when determining the place of the numerous wood fuels in the total family of fuels. It is clear from Table VII that processed wood fuels, such as charcoal and, to some extent pellets, are virtually equal to all other solid fuels available. Other wood fuels, as received by those who would use them directly, are less desirable than coal, but far more useful than the waste materials. They are less concentrated than coal, and the presence of oxygen and water in them significantly reduces their carbon content while presenting other operational problems. However, excepting bark, these fuels are generally higher in carbon content than other biomass fuels, and less problematical from a user point of view. Thus they hold a position in the middle of the fuels spectrum, between coal and wastes. Wood fuels then, are the transition between wastes and coal. Depending upon the degree of processing, they may show proximity to either competitor.

TABLE VII

Analysis of Selected Fuels[a]   (Total Weight As Received)

				Fuel				
Constituent	Bituminous coal[b]	Charcoal (Tech-Air)	Dried sawdust pellets	Maple wood[c]	Douglas fir bark[d]	Bagasse	Municipal waste	Feedlot manure
C	73.2	75.3	47.20	34.0	18.7	30.8	27.5	21.4
H	4.9	3.8	6.49	9.1	2.0	4.0	6.0	2.7
O	4.7	15.2	45.34	28.1	12.2	22.9	36.4	15.6
N	1.2	0.8	0.00	0.2	0.0	0.0	0.5	1.2
S	3.0	0.0	0.00	0.0	Trace	0.0	0.3	0.2
Ash	10.0	3.4	0.97	0.9	0.5	7.3	29.3	8.9
Moisture	3.0	1.5	2.62	32.8	66.6	35.0	20.5	50.0
Btu/lb	13,250	12,090	8,814	6,500	3,000	4,830	4,570	3,090

[a]Sources: [6,7,10,12].

[b]Because of the wide variation in coals, Pittsburgh seam bituminous coal is used as a representative for coal.

[c]Recognizing the similar variation in wood fuels, maple was chosen as representative for cordwood fuels.

[d]This is bark as obtained directly from a wet debarking system.

REFERENCES

1. Fred Shafizadeh and William F. DeGroot, Combustion charac-
    teristics of cellulosic fuels, in Thermal Uses and Proper-
    ties of Carbohydrates and Lignins (Fred Shafizadeh,
    Kyosti V. Sarkanen, and David A. Tillman, eds.). New York:
    Academic Press, 1976.
2. Hermann J. Wenzl, The Chemical Technology of Wood. New York:
    Academic Press, 1970.
3. Roger A. Arola, Wood fuels—how do they stack up? in Energy
    and the Wood Products Industry, Proc. Madison, Wisconsin:
    Forest Products Research Society, 1976.
4. John G. Riley, Development of a small institutional heating
    plant to utilize forest residue fuels. Presented at the
    North Atlantic Region, American Society of Agricultural
    Engineers, New Brunswick, New Jersey, Aug. 15-18, 1976.
5. Stanley E. Corder, Wood and Bark as Fuel, Research Bull. 14.
    Corvallis, Oregon: Oregon State University, August, 1973.
6. J. A. Knight et al., Pyrolytic conversion of agricultural
    wastes to fuels. Presented at the 1974 Annual Meeting of
    the American Society of Agricultural Engineers, Stillwater,
    Oklahoma, June 23-26, 1974.
7. L. L. Anderson, A wealth of waste: A shortage of energy,
    in Fuels From Waste (L. L. Anderson and D. A. Tillman, eds.).
    New York: Academic Press, 1977.
8. M. D. Schlesinger, W. S. Sanner, and D. E. Wolfson,
    Pyrolysis of waste materials from urban and rural sources,
    in Mineral Waste Utilization 1972, Proc. (Murray Schwartz,
    ed.). Chicago, Illinois: Illinois Institute of Tech-
    nology Research Institute and U.S. Bureau of Mines, 1972.
9. C. F. Hawley, Combustion of wood, in Wood Chemistry (2nd
    ed.), Vol. 2 (Louis E. Wise and Edwin C. John, eds.).
    New York: Reinhold, 1952.

10. C. Y. Wen *et al.*, Production of low Btu gas involving coal
     pyrolysis and gasification, in Coal Gasification (Lester G.
     Massey, ed.). Washington, D.C.: American Chemical Society,
     1974.

11. Irving Wender, Fred Steffgen, and Paul Yavorsky, Clean
     liquid and gaseous fuels from organic solid wastes, in
     Recycling and Disposal of Solid Wastes (T. F. Yen, ed.).
     Ann Arbor, Michigan: Ann Arbor Science, 1974.

12. David A. Tillman, Mixing urban waste for gasification in a
     Purox reactor, in Thermal Uses and Properties of Carbohy-
     drates and Lignins, (Fred Shafizadeh, Kyosti V. Sarkanen,
     and David A. Tillman, eds.). New York: Academic Press,
     1976.

13. W. G. Wilson *et al.*, Alkali carbonate and nickel catalysis
     of coal-steam gasification, in Coal Gasification (Lester G.
     Massey, ed.). Washington, D.C.: American Chemical Society,
     1974.

14. Robert T. C. Rasmussen, Advantages of wood-chips and other
     bulky carbonaceous materials in electric smelter charges,
     in Proc. Electric Furnace Conf., 1962. Washington, D.C.:
     The Ferroalloy Assn., 1962.

15. Paul Averitt, Coal, in United States Mineral Resources
     (Donald A. Brobst and Walden P. Pratt, eds.). Washington,
     D.C.: U.S. Geological Survey Professional Paper 820, USGPO,
     1973.

16. Marlies Teichmuller and Rolf Teichmuller, Geological
     causes of coalification, in Coal Science (Robert Gould, ed.).
     Washington, D.C.: American Chemical Society, 1966.

17. Wolfgang Flaig, Chemistry of humic substances in relation
     to coalification, in Coal Science (Robert Gould, ed.).
     Washington, D.C.: American Chemical Society, 1966.

18. T. H. McCulloh, Oil and gas, in United States Mineral
    Resources (Donald A. Brobst and Walden P. Pratt, eds.).
    Washington, D.C.: U.S. Geological Survey Professional
    Paper 820, USGPO, 1973.

19. Fred Shafizadeh and William F. DeGroot, Thermal analysis
    of forest fuels, in Fuels and Energy from Renewable
    Resources (D. A. Tillman, K. V. Sarkanen, and L. L.
    Anderson, eds.). New York: Academic Press, 1977.

20. Arthur Koehler, The Properties and Uses of Wood. New York:
    McGraw-Hill, 1924.

21. Ralph Bogot, Wood as a total energy source. Presented at
    the International Woodworking, Machinery and Furniture
    Supply Fair, Louisville, Kentucky, September 18-22, 1976.

Chapter 4

THE SUPPLY AND DELIVERY
OF WOOD FUELS

I. INTRODUCTION

The perspective most appropriate to examine how wood fuels
fit into the overall energy system is the supply–delivery
approach. This analysis evaluates all stages in the production
system from energy on the ground to energy at the point of
actual use. It includes a careful consideration of extraction
(harvesting), transportation, and energy recovery by combustion
or conversion. In addressing supply–delivery issues, two tasks
are performed simultaneously: (1) providing a description of
the methods and techniques available for acquiring and using
wood fuels, and (2) comparing the energy efficiency of the wood
supply–delivery systems with those appropriate for other
combustible fuels.

The development of comparative energy efficiency values is
complicated by the variety of wood fuels which exist. This
variety includes not only fuel value, as Chapter 3 explains, but
also physical condition and location. For example, wood standing as trees must be harvested, then transported to the point of
use, and then either burned or converted into an alternative
fuel form (e.g., charcoal). Logging residue need not be harvested but it must be transported if it is to be used. Sawmill
waste, spent pulping liquor, and other mill residues do not need

to be harvested or transported. They are ready for use when they become fuel. The extreme case is manufacturing residues in downstream plants (e.g., furniture mills). These fuels are already harvested, transported, and dried. The production of material goods has paid the energy costs to that point. Thus, comparison of wood fuels to fossil fuels is complicated by the variety of existing and potential wood fuels.

The real question that needs to be answered by these supply-delivery analyses, however, is not, "Which fuel is best or most efficient?" Such a question assumes maintaining economic dependence on one or a few fuels, an approach that is self-defeating. Rather, the key question is, "Within what geographical and technical boundaries or parameters are wood fuels most useful?" To approach this issue, comparisons are made with fossil fuels at each juncture of the supply-delivery system. A total comparison is then made employing trajectory analysis.

II.   EXTRACTION OF WOOD FOR FUEL

Extraction costs must be considered if the wood fuel in question exists as a forest. The extraction process for wood standing as trees is harvesting, which distinguishes it initially from coal, oil, natural gas, uranium, and the other energy supplies interred in the earth's crust. Wood extraction is as mechanized as the pursuit and extraction of fossil fuels. It can be accomplished by traditional methods of felling, delimbing, skidding, and assembling logs for transport. It can also be accomplished by complete tree-chipping operations, where trees are felled and fed into in-woods hoggers, which reduce all of the biomass into chips that can be moved by van to the point of utilization.

There are two components associated with the energy costs of each method of extraction: (1) the energy invested in the manufacture of harvesting equipment (e.g., chain saws), and

(2) energy expended in the operation of that machinery. Each machine has a separate energy investment, life expectancy, and hence equipment energy cost per 10^{15} Btu of energy produced. Further, each piece of machinery has a distinct operating (energy) cost. Smith and Corcoran [1] have calculated these capital and operating energy costs per machine and per ton of oven-dry wood produced. These costs, for selected machines, are presented in Table I.

For an overall picture, the costs in Table I must be converted into total extraction energy costs per 10^{15} Btu produced. Then for comparative purposes, one can consider the extraction

TABLE I

Investment and Operating Energy Costs of Selected Equipment per O.D. Ton Produced [1]

Wood harvesting machine	Energy invested in manufacture of machine[a]	Operating energy required[b]
Chain saw	32	33,000
Feller-buncher	10,350	59,700
Limber-buncher	8,350	57,900
Wheeled skidder	10,400	88,500
Forwarder	11,300	115,000
Wheel loader (residues)	3,400	67,200
Loader	3,900	43,500
Whole tree chipper	9,500	65,500
Small truck (50 miles round trip)	6,700	373,000
Large truck (50 miles round trip)	3,300	187,000

[a]This value is obtained by the following formula: $EI = E_M \div (L \times PR)$, where EI is energy investment per ton of wood O.D. equivalent) harvested, E_M total energy for machine manufacture, L life of machine (in hours), and PR production rate per hour. This factor is also known as "capital subsidy."
[b]This value equals fuel consumption for operating the machine while harvesting 1 ton of wood (O.D. equivalent).

costs of other fuels and compare those values to the extraction
costs for wood. Smith and Corcoran estimate that for traditional
logging 0.025×10^{15} Btu are expended as capital and operating
energy for every 1×10^{15} Btu produced. Similarly 0.022×10^{15}
Btu are spent if whole tree chipping is employed [1]. Hayes has
estimated that in the production of coal $\sim 0.021 \times 10^{15}$ Btu are
expended, and in the production of oil and gas $\sim 0.04 \times 10^{15}$ Btu
are expended, when 1×10^{15} Btu are produced [2]. Necessarily
those values represent the weighted averages of expenditures
incurred in U.S. operations.

It is clear that on an extraction basis wood competes evenly
with the fossil fuels. The implication is that on a transportation free basis wood fuel can compete with the more concentrated
energy forms at the plant gate.

III.   THE TRANSPORTATION OF WOOD FUEL

The transportation issue is far more complex thant the extraction issue. Fuels may be transported in numerous ways, and the
costs of different transport modes vary significantly. Further,
transport limits the volume of fuel which can be assembled in
one place.

One presentation of these costs was made by Hottel and
Howard [3]. They showed coal costs as high as $0.14/10^{6}$ Btu
per hundred miles moved by rail, and oil costs as low as
$0.01/10^{6}$ Btu per hundred miles by pipeline. Thirring [4] calculated the transportation radius at which the price of fuel
doubles, demonstrating that during the 1950s cord wood fuel
transported 100 miles by rail would double in price.

The emphasis here, however, is energy cost rather than dollar
cost. To arrive at the effective transportation radius for wood
fuels, three cases were employed. In case A, a direct comparison
with coal was used. Since, on average, 1.32% of the energy in
coal (equivalent) is used to transport that fuel, it was assumed

that 1.32% of the energy in as-harvested wood (equivalent) would
be available for transport. In case B, the weighted average of
energy equivalents used to transport fossil fuels to their first
customer,[1] some 2.15% was used. In case C, 3% was employed since
it is the highest average energy consumption for fuels transport,
occurring in the case of natural gas [2].

The transportation of wood fuels was calculated for truck,
rail, and barge transport. It was calculated recognizing that
the overwhelming majority of wood fuel is transported in 20 ton
truck loads, while a minor fraction of wood fuel moves by rail
[5]. The energy costs of various transportation methods were
obtained from the final report of the National Commission on
Materials Policy [6]. The results of these three calculations
are presented in Table II. All of these energy costs were
calculated for a variety of wood fuels: harvested softwood
(∿45% moisture), harvested hardwood (∿35% moisture), softwood
dried to 15% moisture, and dry charcoal.

The three cases considered plus the variety of fuels provide
measures sensitive to regional differences. In case A, wood and
coal are assumed to be immediately available within the region.
This condition occurs in Appalachia, parts of the southeast
(e.g., Alabama), and parts of the Rocky Mountains. Case B
approximates a national average. Case C approximates conditions
where wood is the only indigenous fuel, and where all fossil
fuels must be imported from points relatively distant from the
region. New England is one such area.

Although not presented in Table II, the energy cost of transportation of wood along the inland and intercoastal waterways
has also been calculated. Energy costs for such barging operations suggest a transportation radius of 250 to 500 miles, a

[1]In the case of coal this could be a power plant or steel
mill; in the case of oil it is the refinery.

Table II

Effective Trans ortation Radii for Wood Fuels

Fuel	Transport method	Energy available for transport (as a % of total energy content)	Effective transport radius (in miles)
Softwood (∿45% moisture)	Truck	1.3	20
		2.2	30
		4.0	40
	Rail	1.3	70
		2.2	110
		4.0	150
Hardwood (∿35% moisture)	Truck	1.3	25
		2.2	40
		4.0	50
	Rail	1.3	90
		2.2	150
		4.0	200
Softwood pellets (∿15% moisture)	Truck	1.3	30
		2.2	60
		4.0	90
	Rail	1.3	120
		2.2	200
		4.0	260
Charcoal	Truck	1.3	60
		2.2	100
		4.0	170
	Rail	1.3	220
		2.2	370
		4.0	490

radius significantly greater than those for truck or rail.   Under
normal circumstances, wood could be used to fuel a power plant
of 50 to 150 megawatts (MW).

Energy efficiency, in the case of fuel transportation has
been used as a constant factor.   This was done in order to estimate transportation distances within which wood can compete.
Through the use of such constants, interfuel comparisons can be
made.   These comparisons are depicted in Fig. 1, employing the
national average of energy expended for fuel transportation:
2.15%.   In Fig. 1, the predominant mode of transportation is
used, along with a major alternative.   In the case of wood,
barging by waterway is also shown.

From these data one can conclude that the normal competitive
radius for wood is about 8% of the competitive radius for coal
and 1.4% of that for oil.   It is also clear that the wastes
represented by municipal refuse have only immediately local
application.   This transportation limitation implies that power
plants or other fuel consuming installations must be far smaller
if fueled by wood than if fueled by coal or oil (e.g., 150 MW
versus 1100 MW).

It is recognized that factors outside the energy arena also
impact on transportation cost.   Those factors have not been
considered here.   Yet a comparison with other studies finds substantial agreement on a ∿50 mile radius for the movement of wood
fuels.   That number has been employed by Smith and Corcoran [1],
Zerbe [8], Battelle Columbus Laboratories [9], and several
others.   Thus the energy budget approach offers a good approximation of the effective transportation radius of fuels.   It
documents that wood is competitive, within specific geographic
areas, with the fossil fuels.

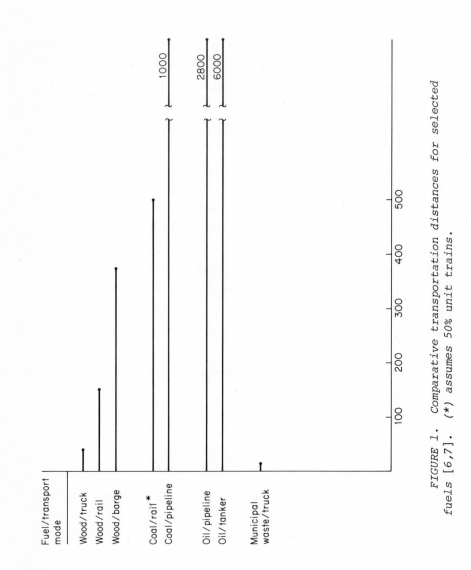

FIGURE 1.   Comparative transportation distances for selected fuels [6,7].   (*) assumes 50% unit trains.

IV. WOOD COMBUSTION SYSTEMS

Recovering the energy value from wood involves either direct combustion or conversion to gaseous or solid fuels followed by combustion of those energy products. In either case the process begins by pyrolysis. This initial pyrolysis drives off the volatiles from the wood which, when reacted with oxygen, burns in flaming combustion as Fig. 2 shows. The simplified reaction model of energy production also shows char or fixed-carbon formation followed by glowing combustion. The fundamental difference between combustion and conversion systems can be seen from Fig. 2. In combustion systems, the reactions all occur in the same reactor: the firebox. In conversion, there is a pyrolysis reactor followed possibly by more conversion systems and then by the combustors.

Three basic approaches exist for complete combustion of wood: (1) the Dutch oven, (2) the spreader-stoker, and (3) the fluidized bed combustor. Each system seeks to achieve complete oxidation of the volatiles plus the fixed carbon in the wood fuels. The reactions detailed in Table III are used to oxidize the char. Where reaction (2) occurs, reaction (3) then occurs to convert the carbon monoxide into carbon dioxide and complete the oxidation process.

TABLE III

Combustion Reactions of Wood Fuels [10]

Reaction	Molecular heat of reaction
(1) $C + O_2 \longrightarrow CO_2$	97.65
(2) $2C + O_2 \longrightarrow 2CO$	58.80
(3) $2CO + O_2 + \longrightarrow 2CO_2$	136.40

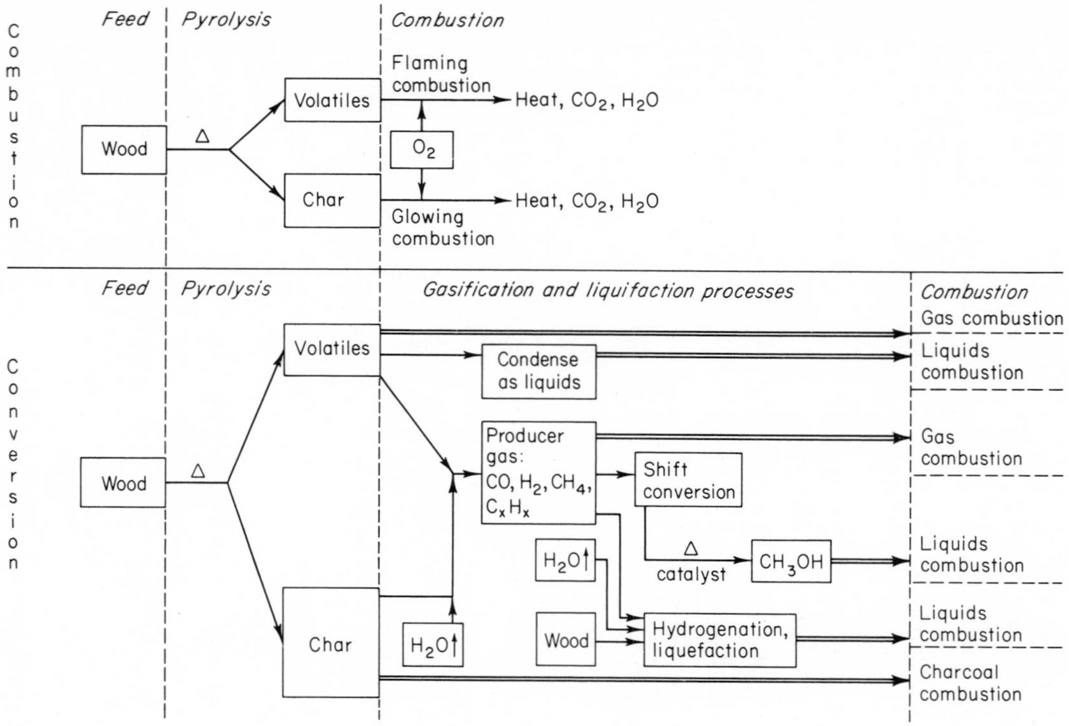

FIGURE 2. *Wood-based energy recovery systems.*

The three combustion systems seek to maximize the oxidation processes while providing (1) flexibility of furnace operations, (2) wet fuels handling, and (3) pollution control from stack gas emissions.

A. *Basic Combustion System Descriptions*

The descriptions provided here are brief overviews. More complete discussions of the Dutch oven and spreader stoker can be found in papers by Voss [11] and the proceedings volume, Energy in the Wood Products Industry [5]. Fluidized bed combustion is described in numerous papers, including that of Smithson [12]. Other papers on fluidized bed combustion are provided in the proceedings previously cited (see reference 5). Discussions presented here are based upon those references.

In the Dutch oven system a heavy bed of wood is placed on the combustor grate. Underfire air flows through the grate to the fuel on the bed, where some combustion occurs. Volatiles given off by the heating of the bed are combusted, above the grate, with overfire air. The fixed carbon is oxidized, incompletely for the most part, and the subsequent combustion of gaseous CO provides much of the energy production from this system.

The spreader-stoker system is now the principal wood burning system employed. In semisuspension burning, the fuel is introduced into the fire box above the grate and begins burning as it falls to the grate. Moisture contained in the fuel is driven off partially when the fuel is in suspension and partially on the grate. The moisture content of the fuel determines the depth of the fuel bed. Because of the design, spreader stokers achieve more complete oxidation, while dutch oven combustors achieve more partial oxidation with the subsequent carbon monoxide burning. The difference is one of degree rather than kind,

however. Some gasification occurs in the spreader-stoker,
depicted as a total combustion system in Fig. 3.

The fluidized-bed combustion system employs a hot bed of
inert material such as sand. The wood is fed into the bed of
sand and preheated combustion air is fed through the grate below
at a velocity sufficient to fluidize the sand and expand its
volume but not to obtain blow-out. The Russian word for fluidized bed combustor translates into "boiling bed" combustion,

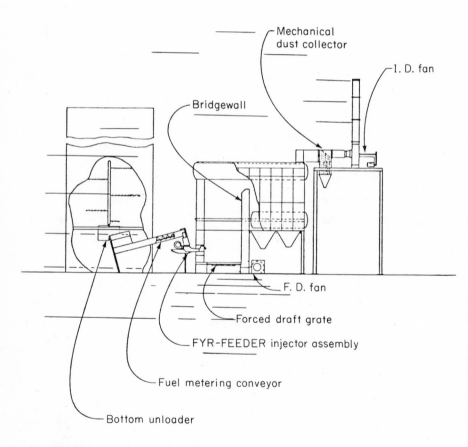

*FIGURE 3. A typical total wood combustion system (drawing
courtesy of American Fyr-Feeder Engineers).*

an apt description of the appearance of such a system in operation. In fluidized-bed combustion, the abrasive inert bed material constantly removes the charred surface of the wood fuel,
exposing fresh material for oxidation. It also retains the fuel
in the bed until combustion is complete.

In addition to the general wood-burning systems described
above, specialized equipment exists for burning sawdust. Again
such equipment partially gasifies the feed material while
completing combustion of the fixed carbon on the grates. One
such design, marketed by American Fyr-Feeder Engineers, is
depicted in Fig. 4. It can handle either sawdust or hogged fuel.

There are numerous designs for each type of combustion system. Such variations involve feeding devices, types of travel-
ing grates for spreader-stoker furnaces, etc. Some one-third of
all boiler manufacturers now provide wood combustors; thus the
range of options is large indeed.

B. Combustion Efficiency of Wood Fuels

Combustion efficiency is determined not only by the extent
to which the oxidation reactions are carried out, but also by the
moisture content and the related issue of the volume of excess
air required to ensure complete combustion. The calculations of
combustion efficiency are made by the following general
formula [13]:

$$CE = \frac{NHV - [w_g \times \text{sp. ht.} \times (t_2 - t_1)] + L_r}{FV} \times 100$$

where CE is the combustion efficiency (%), NHV the net heating
value of incoming wood (Btu/lb), w_g the weight of stack gas (lb),
sp. ht. the specific heat, t_1 the temperature of incoming air
(°F), t_2 the temperature of stack gas (°F), and L_r the radiation
loss (normally ~4%).

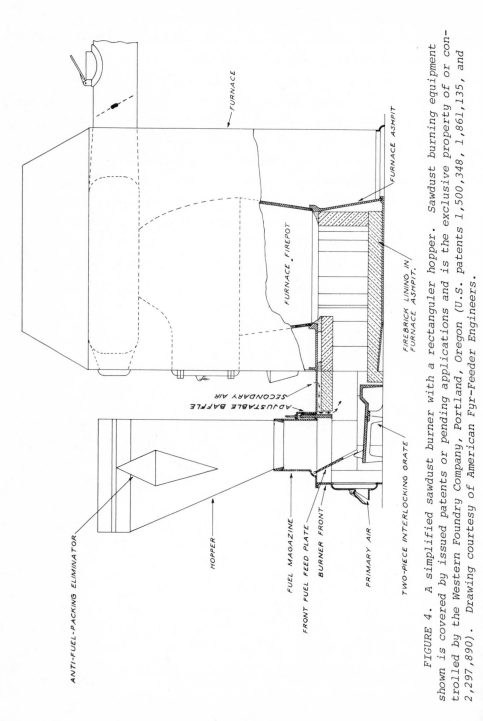

FIGURE 4. A simplified sawdust burner with a rectangular hopper. Sawdust burning equipment shown is covered by issued patents or pending applications and is the exclusive property of or controlled by the Western Foundry Company, Portland, Oregon (U.S. patents 1,500,348, 1,861,135, and 2,297,890). Drawing courtesy of American Fyr-Feeder Engineers.

Labels in figure:
- FURNACE
- FURNACE ASHPIT
- FURNACE FIREPOT
- FIREBRICK LINING IN FURNACE ASHPIT.
- ADJUSTABLE BAFFLE
- SECONDARY AIR
- ANTI-FUEL-PACKING ELIMINATOR
- HOPPER
- FUEL MAGAZINE
- FRONT FUEL FEED PLATE
- BURNER FRONT
- PRIMARY AIR
- TWO-PIECE INTERLOCKING GRATE

The influence of moisture can be observed readily from this formula. Not only does it decrease *NHV* but it also increases w_g, in two ways: It adds moisture to the stack gas, and it also increases the need for excess air to ensure complete oxidation of the fuel. The above formula shows the utility of maximizing heat extraction from the combustion gases to reduce t_2, and of preheating the combustion air (possibly with exhaust air) to raise t_1. Corder [14] has calculated the influence of moisture content on boiler efficiency. The results are presented in column 3 of Table IV, assuming a 400°F stack gas temperature, and then extended to show the energy delivery implications.

TABLE IV

The Influence of Moisture on Fuel Value and Combustion Efficiency

Moisture content as-received basis (%)	Fuel value softwood (Btu/lb)	Thermal efficiency at 400°F stack temp. (%) [14]	Net energy produced per lb wood burned (Btu)
0.0	8800	81	7130
16.7	7125	78	5560
28.6	5930	75	4480
37.5	5040	72	3630
44.4	4345	70	3040
50.0	3785	68	2575
54.5	3333	66	2200
58.3	2950	63	1860
61.5	2630	60	1580
64.3	2350	57	1340
66.7	2110	55	1160

The summary of these data, the influence of moisture content
on fuel value and net energy delivered are recast here as Fig. 5.
It shows the influence of wood moisture content, when calculated
on an as-received basis, to be a linear function. For the
influence on net heat content, the equation is: E_n = 8800
- 100.28M, where E_n represents the net energy value in Btu/lb,
8800 represents the dry weight energy content, and M represents
% moisture. For the net energy delivered per lb of wood combusted, the equation is E_d = 7130 - 89.29M where E_d represents
energy delivered as steam, 7130 represents the net energy delivered at 0% moisture (per lb of wood combusted), and M represents
% moisture. Fig. 5 shows the slight divergence of these func-
tions as the feedstock wood becomes progressively dryer. More
importantly, it shows the rapid deterioration in the utility of
wood as a fuel as it becomes progressively more moisture laden.

It is the judgment of numerous expert individuals that pre-
drying of wood does not solve overall system efficiency problems,
since energy is consumed in the drying process, low-grade oxidation occurs, and some pollution may result [15]. Thus if one
assume hardwood fuel with 35% moisture (total weight basis) as
Chapter 3 suggests, and if one operates with an average stack
temperature of 400°F, one can utilize that hardwood at above
72% energy recovery efficiency. For 45% moisture softwoods, the
average efficiency is slightly less than 70%.

The delivery of useful heat is critical to the economic
value of a fuel, and combustion efficiency is one essential parameter in that determination. Thus it is useful to compare the
combustion efficiency of wood with that of coal, oil, natural
gas, and municipal waste. Only with these data can total energy
supply-delivery trajectories be developed.

The standard combustion efficiency quoted for pulverized
coal is 80-85%. A similar range can be cited for natural gas
and fuel oil. The combustion efficiency range cited for wood
is 67-72%. A comparable steam raising efficiency for municipal

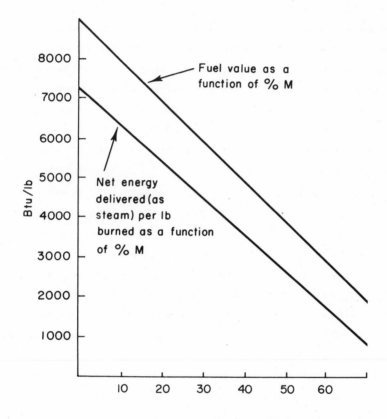

FIGURE 5.   Net heating value and net energy delivery capability of wood as a function of moisture content.

waste combustion (incineration with heat recovery) is about 55%
(52-58%) [17]. For many of the low carbon content wastes
(e.g., sewage sludge at 20% solids) the heat released by combustion about equals the energy required to vaporize the water
content [12]. Thus wood, which is normally combusted at 67-72%
efficiency, is a highly useful fuel. It should be noted that
Grace puts the thermal efficiency of spent liquor recovery
furnaces at 38.5-40.5% [18]. These furnaces, of course, must
accomplish chemical recovery as well as energy recovery and are
not optimized solely towards Btu production.

V.   CONVERSION OF WOOD TO ALTERNATIVE FUEL FORMS

    In years gone by, wood was burned directly, converted into
charcoal, and converted into producer gas. Chapter 1 detailed
the past use of conversion systems in this country and abroad.
With the advent of cheap petroleum and natural gas, however,
such systems fell into disfavor and were ultimately abandoned.
Today, we are rediscovering this approach to recovering the
energy values from wood. A new conversion industry is in its
infancy. This rebirth is occurring in order to meet the needs
for a broader supply of fuels.
    There are several generic approaches to conversion: pyroly-
sis, gasification, hydrogenation, enzymatic hydrolysis followed
by fermentation, and anaerobic digestion. Pyrolysis yields
several products in solid, liquid, and gaseous forms. This
technique, employed by the Ford Motor Co. (see Chapter 1) during
the 1920s, is now particularly advanced and will be discussed
further here. Gasification involves producing a low or medium
Btu gas by pyrolysis plus water-gas shift reactions. It is also
reemerging. Hydrogenation, the technique pioneered by the
German Nobel prize winning chemist Bergius in the 1920s and
1930s, is employed to produce liquid fuels from coal. For several reasons it is being applied to wood in research today.

Fermentation and digestion, while appropriate generally to biomass, are not particularly well suited to energy recovery from
wood and receive no further treatment here. In this presentation,
the major approaches to conversion are described, employing specific examples where appropriate. Overall system efficiencies
are provided in order to facilitate comparative analysis.

A. *Pyrolysis*

Pyrolysis consists of the destructive distillation of organic
material in the absence of oxygen. The initial products of wood
pyrolysis, as shown in Fig. 2, are volatiles and carbonaceous
char. Part of the gas stream exiting any pyrolysis reactor con-
denses into a liquid, or synthetic oil. It may be burned as such
or upgraded into chemical feedstocks.

There are many pyrolysis schemes extant, each designed to
maximize production of one or another fuel. Of particular importance to the wood industry is the Tech-Air Process. This system,
developed at the Georgia Institute of Technology, is a fixed-bed,
low-temperature (1100°F) system. The largest installation is a
50 TPD unit at a sawmill in Cordele, Georgia. The schematic of
that unit is depicted here as Fig. 6. The Cordele installation
is shown in Fig. 7.

In the Tech-Air process, incoming wood residue is dried with
waste heat and a portion of the noncondensible gas stream from
pyrolysis. From there the dry residue ($\sim$5% moisture) is charged
to the pyrolysis reactor, where char and gas are produced.
Partial oxidation of the incoming feed material supplies the
heat necessary to drive the reactions. The char is collected
immediately, while the gas is passed through an off-gas cyclone
and a condenser. There oils and water are collected. The noncondensible power gas is then passed to a boiler, with a portion
being segregated for use in drying the incoming waste [19,20].

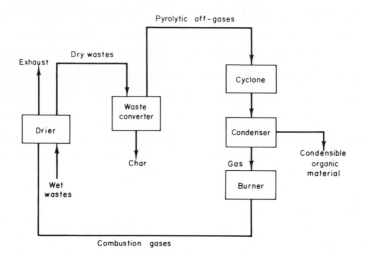

FIGURE 6.   Block diagram of Tech-Air process.

FIGURE 7.   The 50 ton/day Tech-Air installation at Cordele, Georgia.   (Photo courtesy of Georgia Institute of Technology.)

The mix of energy products from this process varies with the operating temperature of the retort. Table V summarizes the volume and energy content of the products produced per ton of dry input ton. The char has an energy content of ∿13,000 Btu/lb [21], the oil has ∿3.88 million Btu/bbl (∿9900 Btu/lb) [22], and the gas has ∿300 Btu/ft^3 (∿5000 Btu/lb) [21]. Table V should not be construed as an energy efficiency calculation since it does not include the energy input to the system (e.g., electricity to run motors) and it does not discount the gas used for drying the incoming waste. It is estimated that the net thermal efficiency of this system is ∿80%.

B. *Gasification*

Gasification is a major modification of fundamental pyrolysis. As with pyrolysis, initially the product streams are gaseous volatiles and char. However, in gasification, the reactions are carried out at sufficiently high temperatures to limit the production of condensible tars and oils. If possible, the tars

TABLE V

Energy Production from the Tech-Air Process per Input Ton of Dry Wood [19-22]

Material	Volume of product produced per ton of incoming dry waste	Energy content	Energy produced per incoming ton (of dry wood, 1 × 10^6 Btu)
Char	460 lb	13,000 Btu/lb	5.98
Oil	600 lb	9,900 Btu/lb	5.95
Gas	12,000 ft^3	300 Btu/ft^3	3.57
Total	1,775 lb	N/A	14.50

and oils formed are recycled to the reactor for additional crack-
ing. Further, in gasification, some of the char is partially
oxidized to drive the reactions. The remaining char is reacted
with water to produce additional gaseous compounds. Table VI
details the principal reactions used to gasify the char product
stream.

Gasification reactors may be of fixed-, entrained-, or
fluidized-bed design. Of more significance than vessel config-
uration, however, is the means by which oxygen is supplied for
partial combustion of the char to drive the gasification reactions. Some systems, such as the American Fyr-Feeder design,
use air. Others employ pure oxygen.

Air blown systems, as Table VII shows, produce a gas that is
high in nitrogen content. This requires an immediate coupling
of the gasifier and the combustor in order to permit recovery of
the sensible heat contained in the nitrogen. Air-blown gasification requires air preheaters but not expensive oxygen generation equipment. On the other hand, oxygen-blown gasification
produces a higher energy value fuel ($\sim$350 Btu/ft^3), which may be

Table VI

Reactions of Wood Gasification [10]

Reaction	Molecular heat of reaction
(1) $C + O_2 \longrightarrow CO_2$	+ 97.65
(2) $2C + O_2 \longrightarrow 2CO$	+ 58.8
(3) $C + CO_2 \longrightarrow 2CO$	- 38.8
(4) $C + H_2O \longrightarrow CO + H_2$	- 28.8
(5) $C + 2H_2O \longrightarrow CO_2 + 2H_2$	- 18.8

TABLE VII

Comparison of the Fuel Values of Wood, Gas, and Methane [11,17]

Parameter chemical composition (wt %)	Gaseous Fuel Product		
	Air-fed system gas	Oxygen-fed system gas	Natural gas
H_2	10	24.0	–
CO	30	40.0	–
CH_4	1	5.6	96.0
$C_2-C_6H_x$	3	4.4	3.0
H_2S	–	0.05	–
CO_2	6	25.0	0.2
N	50	–	0.8
Other	–	0.95	–
Total	100.0	100.0	100.0
Lower heating value (Btu/ft^3)	∿200	∿350	1026

cooled and stored for short periods of time without significant energy losses. Furthermore, the gas produced by oxygen-fed reactors may be transported over modest distances.

Gasification may be performed on wood chunks, chips, sawdust, or bark. Of particular importance to the forest industries is the Lacotte process for gasifying relatively large pieces of wood of modest moisture (20-30%, as-received basis). This process, developed by de Lacotte of France, is depicted schematically in Fig. 8 and compared to standard gasifier designs. Wood is fed into the top of a vertical retort and passes through three operational zones: (1) drying, (2) pyrolysis, and (3) char gasification. Volatiles driven off from the initial reactions are taken off at the top of the reactor and passed

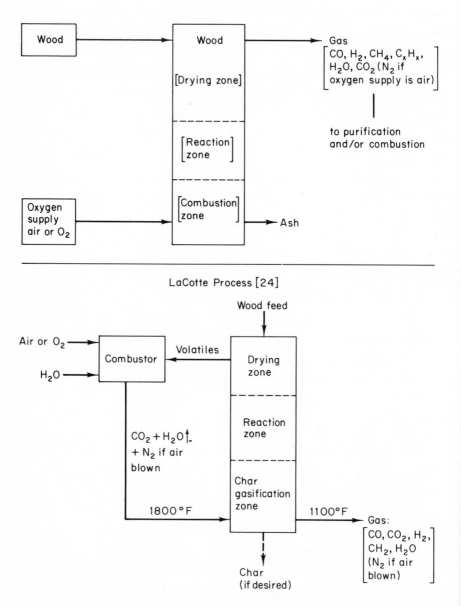

FIGURE 8. A comparison of standard gasification and the Lacotte process.

to a combustor fed with air or oxygen plus steam. The products
from that combustion are fed into the bottom of the retort at
1800°F (1000°C) to supply heat and steam for the operation of the
reaction vessel. The principal gas stream is withdrawn from the
base of the reactor at 1100°F (600°C). Char may be withdrawn or
completely gasified [23]. Because of the high temperatures of
reaction, tars and other condensibles are completely destroyed,
simplifying equipment maintenance and environmental protection.
There is no apparent need for gas scrubbing with attendant water
pollution problems. The gaseous product is a mixture of CO_2, CO,
H_2, CH_4, H_2, and H_2O. Its heating value is ~200 Btu/ft^3 if the
combustor is fed with air and ~300 Btu/ft^3 if the combustor is
fed with oxygen. The thermal efficiency of this system is
70-75%, depending upon the form in which oxygen is supplied to
the combustor [23].

Overall thermal efficiency of gasification has been calculated for numerous systems. Brink [24], using perhaps the most
rigorous analysis, has placed air-blown gasification system
efficiency (including combustion to raise steam) at 78.4%, and
oxygen-blown system efficiency at 81.3%. As Brink's analysis
shows, however, gasification efficiency is as vulnerable to
increasing moisture content as combustion efficiency.

C. Liquefaction

The production of such energy forms from wood and other biomass sources has been given a great deal of exposure in the
literature. The production of methanol has received particular
attention with some authors pointing to its ubiquity in application [25]. Production of heavy oil has received nearly equal
attention. Attention is focused on liquid fuels due to the need
to find substitutes for petroleum. Both the production of light
and heavy liquids will be discussed here, with catalytic hydrogenation being discussed as the method of producing the latter
fuel.

1. Methanol Production. Methanol production is an extension of oxygen-blown gasification as described previously. The
synthesis gas is purified and, by reaction steam, is adjusted to
a volumetric H_2:CO ratio of 2:1. Then in the presence of heat
and a catalyst such as zinc oxide or a mixture of catalysts, the
endothermic reaction

$$CO + 2H_2 \xrightarrow[\text{catalyst}]{\text{heat}} CH_3OH$$

is carried out. A complete description of the production of
methanol from waste is provided by Haider [26]. The methanol so
produced can be employed as a transportation fuel additive, as a
fuel in peaking electric power plants, and in other applications.

Numerous advantages are enjoyed by wood in the preparation of
synthesis gas. These include a relatively high H_2:CO ratio in
the gas *vis-a-vis* coal, reducing the shift requirements; low
desulfurization costs in purifying the gas; and reduced risks of
catalyst poisoning due to the low sulfur content of wood [27].
Despite these advantages, the energy efficiency of methanol production, defined as $\Sigma E_o / \Sigma E_i$ where E_o is total energy output
including byproducts and E_i is all energy inputs including feed
material and auxiliary power, is in the 34-37% range [28].

2. Heavy-Liquids Production. There are two basic systems
for the production of heavy liquids as the sole product of wood
conversion: The Occidental Petroleum pyrolysis system described
by Pober and Bauer [29], and the catalytic hydrogenation process
developed at the Pittsburgh Energy Research Center and being
tested at a pilot plant located in Albany, Oregon (Fig. 9). It
is this latter process that will be dealt with here. Like
methanol production, this process involves extended use of synthesis gas, but there the similarity stops.

The hydrogenation process has been described extensively in
the literature [30-32]. In this process, part of the incoming
wood waste is pyrolyzed to yield synthesis gas. The synthesis

FIGURE 9. The wood to heavy liquids plant of Albany, Oregon. (Photo courtesy of U.S. Department of Energy.)

gas used principally for its CO content, plus steam, is then
reacted with finely ground wood waste in the presence of an alka-
line carbonate catalyst under elevated pressures (1500–3500 psig)
and temperatures (700°F) to accomplish deoxygenation of the wood.
Appell provides the following generation equation for the
process [32]:

$$0.61(C_6H_{9.13}O_{4.33}) + 0.23CO + 0.08H_2$$

$$\xrightarrow[\text{catalyst}]{H_2O} H_2O + 0.64CO_2 + 0.53(C_6H_{6.93}O_{1.22})$$

Heavy oils from lignocellulosic materials are far from
identical to heavy petroleum oils (e.g., #6 oil) as Table VIII
illustrates. They are lower in heating value, acidic, and
exhibit handling characteristics that make them less valuable.
This is true for the catalytic hydrogenation oil produced by the
process described above and for the Occidental Petroleum oil.
Energy efficiencies for producing these oils are in the 33–38%
range. Further, as Appell observes, high lignin content materials such as Douglas Fir bark consume more CO supplied for liquefaction, have lower conversion efficiencies, and have lower
product yields when being processed. Materials that are high in
hemicellulose content are more suitable [32].

D. *Comparative Conversion Efficiencies*

Two types of comparisons merit examination: (1) a comparison of wood combustion and wood conversion systems, and (2) a
comparison of conversion efficiencies between wood and other
candidate feedstocks. From these data, preliminary conclusions
can be drawn concerning candidate systems for trajectory analysis
and deployment.

1. *Wood Fuel Utilization Systems Comparison*. In order to
provide meaningful comparisons, it must be assumed that the
converted fuels are combusted to raise steam. Further, the

TABLE VIII

Heavy Oil Characteristics [22,29,33]

Parameter, elemental analysis	Oil types			
	Catalytic hydrogenation oil	Occidental Petroleum oil	Tech-Air oil	#6 Heating oil
C	77.0	57.5	65.6	85.7
H	10.7	7.6	7.8	10.5
N	2.8	0.9	0.9	} 2.0
O	8.8	33.4	25.6[a]	
S	0.3	0.3	0.1	0.7-3.5
Energy value (Btu/lb)	15,000	10,500	9800	18,200
Specific gravity	0.03	1.30	N/A[b]	0.98
Density lb/gal	8.58	10.85	9.35	8.18
Pumping temp. (°F)	140	160	N/A[b]	115
Atomization temp (°F)	N/A[b]	240	N/A[b]	220

[a]By difference.   [b]Not available.

Tech-Air fuels must be taken together and treated as if they were one fuel. On this basis, Table IX presents the relative energy efficiencies of wood utilization systems.

It should be recognized that the percentages presented are approximations. One cannot come closer, in reality, given the variability in heating value and moisture content of the feed-stock, wood. Further it should be recognized that, as the feed material is increased in moisture content, the small gap between combustion and gasification disappears and may even be reversed as Brink [24] suggests. Similarly it has been shown that pyroly-sis of concentrated spent liquor by the St. Regis process [34]

Table IX

Relative Energy Efficiencies of Wood Utilization Systems

Candidate system	Thermal efficiency before combustion (%)	Thermal efficiency after combustion (%)
Direct combustion	N/A[a]	∿70
Tech-Air multiple product pyrolysis	∿80	∿70
Wood gasification	∿80	∿70
Methanol production	∿35	∿30
Heavy oil production	∿35	∿30

[a]Not applicable.

or the Weyerhauser process [35] is more efficient in energy production than direct combustion of this moisture-laden fuel.
Grace [18] estimates the comparative efficiencies between pyrolysis and combustion at ∿50 and ∿40%, respectively.

It is also clear from Table IX that liquefaction is the least
desirable alternative if the fuel producer has a choice. The
2:1 advantage of combustion and pyrolysis over liquefaction can
not be obliterated by moisture since synthesis gas is essential
to both processes. Liquefaction faces an additional disadvantage: higher capital costs due to the need for pressure vessels
and/or more complex process trains. Thus it will only be
deployed if there is no other energy alternative for wood available to the individual processor, and if wood liquefaction can
compete with the creation of liquid fuels from alternative feedstocks.

2. Wood Conversion Compared to Alternative Feedstocks. The
comparison of one conversion system to another does not depend
upon the combustion adjustment, or even process equivalence, as
much as it depends upon end product equivalence. For this

discussion, the production of industrial gas ($\sim$150–$\sim$450 Btu/ft^3) is treated as one set of comparative data and liquefaction is treated as another.

When one compares gasification of wood to conversion of coal on the one hand and wastes on the other, one finds efficiencies that roughly correspond to positions on the carbon curve posited in Chapter 3. Such comparisons can only be approximate because process configurations vary markedly. For the extremely wet feeds such as manure, anaerobic digestion must be employed. For dryer materials pyrolysis is more appropriate. Still approximate comparisons are useful and for that reason are provided in Table X. The data show that wood enjoys the flexibility of use in its natural form or after conversion into gaseous or diverse pyrolysis fuels. The position of wood liquefaction *vis-a-vis* other fuels, however, is significantly less advantageous. Table XI shows the comparative efficiency of wood conversion to other fuels with oil data coming from Hayes [2], heavy liquids from

TABLE X

Comparative Gasification Efficiences [36-38]

Feedstock	Process	Product (Btu/ft^3 gas)	Thermal efficiency (%)
Coal	Koppers-Totzek (oxygen blown)	$\sim$300	$\sim$88
Coal	Lurgi (air blown)	$\sim$150	$\sim$82
Wood	American Fyr-Feeder (air blown)	$\sim$200	$\sim$78
Municipal waste	Purox (oxygen blown)	$\sim$350	$\sim$66
Manure	Anaerobic digestion	$\sim$500	$\sim$33

TABLE XI

The Energy Efficiency of Producing Liquids from Selected
Feedstocks

| | Liquid | |
	Heavy liquids (%)	Methanol (%)
Feedstock		
Oil	89[a]	–
Coal	74	55
Wood	35	35
Municipal waste	35	33
Manure	–	17

[a]Oil-refining energy expenditure [2].

coal data being reported by Goddard [39], and light-liquid data
coming from Reed [28] and the CORRIM Committee [27].

It is clear from Table XI that wood cannot compete on an
efficiency basis as a feedstock for liquids; the disadvantage
is as great vis-a-vis coal as it is vis-a-vis wood gasification.

There are additional problems with producing liquids from
wood. Katzen, as cited by the CORRIM Committee, has shown that
economies of scale in converting a solid feedstock to methanol
are not available to wood [27]. Coal-to-methanol systems do
benefit from economies of scale, however. Thus in a market where
substantial demand is created for methanol as a transportation
fuel, wood will be at a competitive disadvantage. Similar scale
problems exist when one seeks to produce synthetic petroleum
from wood and coal. In the search for alternative liquid fuels
then, wood will not play any significant role. In general,
conversion of wood to make concentrated fuel forms is desirable, but only if such conversion involves pyrolysis to a range
of products, or gasification.

VI.   OVERALL SUPPLY-DELIVERY EFFICIENCY

A comparative analysis of various fuels must consider energy losses at all stages of the chain of energy supply. It must include efficiencies of extraction, transportation, and recovery by combustion or conversion. It is the synthesis of such efficiency factors that provides for overall supply-delivery assessment. Such an assessment is not made to determine which fuel is best; rather it is to determine within what parameters the fuels compete evenly.

One useful approach to this synthesis is trajectory analysis, a method of energy accounting that isolates and identifies each energy loss and simultaneously provides a means for summing all losses. Trajectory analysis also provides a means for determining which losses are most significant. Furthermore, it provides a means for comparing the degree to which a given fuel supply-delivery chain delivers energy to the ultimate point of use.

Because trajectory analysis provides a mechanism for summarizing the energy efficiencies at all stages in the supply-delivery chain, it provides a means for examining the overall effectiveness of a given fuel within certain assumed parameters. It is particularly useful for it encompasses the entire system, recognizing that losses in any stage must be dealt with. Thus it is employed here to provide a means for drawing conclusions concerning the position of various fuels within the U.S. economic system.

The net output of a fuel can be presented as trajectory efficiency percentage determined by the following formula:[2]

---

[2]The n is used to show possible subsequent steps not analyzed here, e.g., secondary transportation or, if electricity is produced, the energy losses associated with resistance heating, electrical motors, furnaces, etc.

$$E_{sd} = \left(V_h - \sum_{i=1}^{n} C_i \right) / V_h$$

where E_{sd} is the overall efficiency of the specific supply-demand system, V_h the value of fuel as harvested, C_1 the energy cost of harvesting, C_2 the energy cost of transportation, C_3 the energy cost of recovery, C_{3a} the energy cost of conversion, and C_{3b} the energy cost of combustion.

These efficiency percentages can be calculated for all fuels on a direct combustion basis (elimination C_{3a} calculations) or on a conversion followed by combustion basis. Further, if electricity rather than steam is to be the final product, a C_{3c} factor may be added. In handling the energy costs, simple loss calculations are used unless a conversion step is added. In such a case, conversion and combustion are coupled as a recovery system. Electricity generation would be handled in like manner. The formula can also handle transportation after conversion but before final recovery by inserting a second transport element, not shown or used here, between C_{3a} and C_{3b}.

Trajectory analysis is also useful because it lends itself to graphic presentation. Fig. 10 is the trajectory of wood fuel utilizing the following chain of events: whole tree chipping extraction, truck transport (50 miles), gasification, and gas combustion to raise steam. The end-point efficiency percentage is derived from applying the preceding formula.

It should be emphasized that there are neither first nor second law efficiency calculations. The summation is of dissimilar loss types. This is more analogous to energy accounting than engineering. The final numbers presented should be treated as the midpoint in a range of values. For the purposes of this discussion, a state value of 75% should be treated as representative of the range 70-80%.

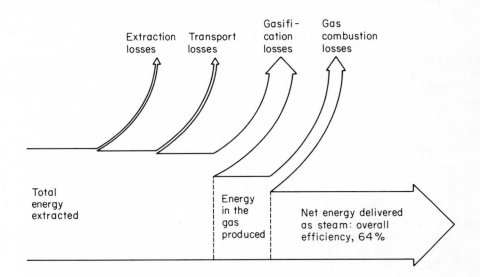

FIGURE 10. Typical trajectory for wood fuel using gasification system approach.

TABLE XII summarizes the efficiency factors developed for each fuel for all stages in the supply–delivery system. These factors do not include liquefaction of coal, wood, or other materials due to the conclusions presented above. It can be seen from Table XII that, statistically, the net result will be most sensitive to changes in the combustion or conversion factors since they generate the most losses. The supply–delivery system is least sensitive to changes in extraction efficiency despite the upstream position of that factor, unless such changes are in orders of magnitude.

The Application of Trajectory Analysis

In this application of trajectory analysis, the total competitive nature of the wood fuel family is examined. Since extraction efficiency when used varies by only 0.3%, it is held

TABLE XII

Energy Efficiency Factors for Various Fuels

Stage in supply-delivery system	Fuel energy efficiency per operation (%)			
	Wood	Coal	Oil	MSW
Extraction	97.8	97.9	96.0	97.0
Transport[a]	97.85	99.6	99.9+	88.2
Transport[b]	97.85	99.4	99.9+	82.2
Direct combustion[c]	65.0-75.0[d]	80.0	N/A	55.0
Conversion	75.0-80.0[d]	85.0	89.0[e]	70.0
Combustion of conversion fuel product (losses of both conversion and combustion)	49.0-65.0[d]	72.0	76.0	60.0

[a]Assumed distance: 50 miles, most frequent mode (e.g., truck for wood).

[b]Assumed distance: 150 miles, optimum mode (e.g., rail for wood).

[c]Includes cost of running emission control equipment including scrubbers for coal.

[d]A range is used here depending on the fuel value and moisture content of the wood assumed to be used.

[e]Oil refining estimate.

constant. The maximum transportation distances by mode of transport, 50 and 200 miles, are employed if other than mill residue fuels are used. Recovery systems are varied between direct combustion and gasification followed by combustion. First, the primary trajectories for wood are presented in Table XIII. These trajectories are then compared, selectively, to the trajectories for other fuels. With this number of parameters, there are over 4000 possible comparisons. This comparative analysis focuses on the following areas: the distinction

between fuels as they are used most commonly and the optimum
trajectory for each fuel. In the comparative trajectories, the
method of energy recovery is held constant between wood, coal,
and municipal solid waste (MSW), except when each fuel is
optimized.

There is no magic cutoff number of minimum overall efficiency
in order to establish the economic viability as a fuel. It is
the author's position that such a cut-off number would be ∿60%.
Given such an assumption, Table XIII shows that wood is reasonably economic at 50 miles, but the options at 200 miles are
highly constrained. Truck transportation is unacceptable. The
utility of conversion is highly dependent on the quality of the
wood feed and the efficiency of the process. It should be noted
that, at 200 miles, a 10% drop in combustion efficiency (to 60%)
eliminates that process also. Because the efficiency of the
wood system does not exceed 67% in any case, the economic accepti-
bility of this fuel is highly sensitive to efficiency losses in
any given parameter. Again the influence of moisture is felt.

The comparison between wood and other fuels begins with a
normal industry practice comparison at 50 miles (Table XIV),
and an individual fuel optimization comparison at 50 miles
(Table XV). In all of these comparisons oil is refined before
use; hence the conversion step there. Fig. 11 provides a normalized comparison between harvested wood and coal, again to depict
visually the delivery energy at the point of utilization.

TABLE XIII

Trajectories for the Supply-Delivery of Wood Fuels (Assumes extraction or availability of 1×10^{12} Btu in wood fuels; values expressed in 10^9 Btu)

Parameter	Residue trajectories		
	Manufacturing residue[b]	Mill residue[c]	Logging residue[d]
Energy cost of extraction	0	0	0
Energy cost of transport	0	0	22
Energy cost of conversion	0	0	0
Energy cost of combustion	190	280	656
Net energy delivered (as steam)	810	720	344
Net energy efficiency	81	72	66

[a] Harvest of wood for fuel might occur if mixed stands are being converted to plantations.

[b] Assumes bone dry material in a furniture plant.

[c] Assumes moisture content of 35-40%.

[d] Assumes residue to be 50% moisture. Haul distance of 30 miles assumed. Haul method, truck.

TABLE XIII (Continued)

Harvest trajectories[a]		
Truck transport (30 mi) direct combustion[e]	Truck transport (30 mi) pyrolysis[f]	Rail transport (110 mi) direct combustion[g]
25	25	25
22	22	22
0	200	0
300	120	300
653	633	653
65	63	65

[e]Assumes harvesting of scrub pine plus hardwoods at average moisture content of 35–45%.

[f]Assumes same wood as in note e. Assumes Tech-Air conversion and 85% efficiency on combustion of products (e.g., charcoal).

[g]This case is identical to harvest-truck-combustion. It shows rail radius.

TABLE XIV

The Normalized Energy Trajectory at 50 Mile Radius, Harvesting
and Using 10^{12} Btu

Parameter (in 10^9 Btu)	Fuel			
	Wood	Coal	Oil	MSW
Tons extracted	76,900	42,600	26,300	104,200
Energy cost of extraction	25.0	21.3	40.0	29.8
Energy cost of transport	22.0	2.2	0.4	59.5
Energy cost of conversion	–	–	110	–
Energy cost of combustion	300	200	130	450
Net energy delivered	653	776.5	720	460.7
Net energy efficiency (%)	65.3	77.7	72.0	46.1

TABLE XV

Individual Fuel Optimization at 50 Miles, Extracting and
Using 10^{12} Btu

Parameter (in 10^9 Btu)	Fuel			
	Wood	Coal	Oil	MSW
Energy cost of extraction	22[a]	21.3	40	29.8
Energy cost of transportation	5.7[b]	1.2[c]	0.4[c]	59.5
Energy cost of conversion	–	–	110	300[d]
Energy cost of combustion	300	200	130	100
Net energy delivered	672.3	777.5	719.6	510.7
Net energy efficiency (%)	67.2	78.0	72.0	51.1

[a] Assumes whole tree chipping for harvest optimization.

[b] Assumes rail transportation.

[c] Assumes pipeline transportation.

[d] Conversion used as it is more efficient; Purox process assumed.

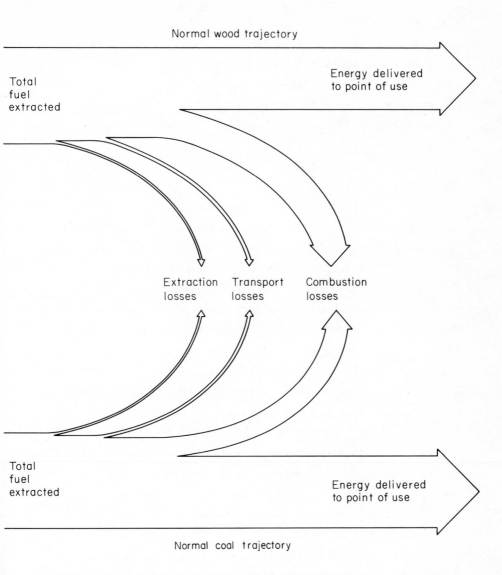

Normal wood trajectory

Total
fuel
extracted

Energy delivered
to point of use

Extraction
losses

Transport
losses

Combustion
losses

Total
fuel
extracted

Energy delivered
to point of use

Normal coal trajectory

FIGURE 11.   Comparison of normal wood and coal trajectories.

VII. CONCLUSIONS

Wood fuels are desirable sources of energy, and can be used
relatively efficiently if the following conditions hold:
(1) extraction costs are minimized; (2) transportation distances
are held down to 30 to 50 miles; and (3) energy recovery processes
employed are direct combustion, pyrolysis, or gasification. It
is a matter of selecting the right wood fuel and the right
supply-delivery system to meet the needs of an appropriate application (e.g., raising steam for a pulp mill). The advantages for
using wood fuels in an optimum situation are great; concomitantly
the penalties for selecting the wrong use and the wrong supply-
delivery system (e.g., liquefaction) are severe.

There is a gradient of fuel efficiencies starting with the
furniture or wood products plants where wood competes evenly with
fossil fuels, and moving rapidly downward through forest industry
mill residues to logging residues and to harvested materials.
That curve of declining efficiency, combined with the rising total
cost of using fossil fuels, determines the extent to which
various wood fuels are competitive. Forest fuels will become
economically competitive when the cost differential between them
and fossil fuels exceeds the efficiency differential. That disparity ultimately will make logging residues and some harvested
woods competitive if the elements of the supply-delivery system
are properly aligned and the end use for the wood fuel is
appropriate.

The extent to which various wood fuels (e.g., logging residues) become competitive will be determined locally. In areas
such as northern New England, where fossil fuels must be
imported from sources several hundred miles away (e.g., coal
from Pennsylvania, natural gas from Louisiana), many wood fuels
are now highly attractive. In regions where indigenous fossil
energy sources abound (e.g., Montana), only the better grades of
wood fuel can compete. Such regional differences result from

transportation energy costs reducing and ultimately obliterating, or reinforcing, energy recovery efficiency differences between wood and the fossil fuels.

The competitive position of wood is more economically influenced relatively by incremental recovery efficiency gains than is the position of coal. Wood is closer to the competitive/ not competitive boundary. Further, efficiency involves loss minimization. For this reason wood is a prime candidate for energy recovery systems such as cogeneration, systems which focus on maximizing energy recovery and minimizing losses. Because wood fuels are prime candidates for such advanced deployment systems, it is time to turn our attention to them.

REFERENCES

1. Norman Smith and Thomas J. Corcoran, The energy analysis of wood production for fuel applications, *in* Symposium on Net Energetics of Integrated Synfuel Systems (Preprints). Washington, D.C.: American Chemical Society (Fuels Division), April, 1976.

2. Earl T. Hayes, Energy implications of materials processing, Science 191, Feb. 20, 1976.

3. H. C. Hottel and J. B. Howard, New Energy Technology—Some Facts and Assessments. Cambridge, Mass.: MIT Press, 1971.

4. Hans Thirring, Energy for Man. New York: Harper and Row (Colophon Edition), 1976. (Original U.S. publication, Indiana Univ. Press, 1958.)

5. Einak B. Hoff, Handling of forest products fuels, *in* Energy and the Wood Products Industry. Madison, Wisconsin: The Forest Products Research Society, 1976.

6. National Commission on Materials Policy, Material Needs and the Environment Today and Tomorrow. Washington, D.C.: USGPO, June, 1973.

7. Task Force on Energy, U.S. Energy Prospects: An Engineering Viewpoint. Washington, D.C.: National Academy of Science, 1974.

8. John I. Zerbe, Conversion of stagnated timber stands to productive sites using noncommercial material for fuel, in Fuels and Energy From Renewable Resources (D. A. Tillman, K. V. Sarkanen, and L. L. Anderson, eds.). New York: Academic Press, 1977.

9. Battelle Columbus Laboratories, Comparison of Fossil and Wood Fuels. Washington, D.C.: U.S. Environmental Protection Agency, 1976.

10. N. E. Rambush, Modern Gas Producers. New York: Van Nostrand, 1922.

11. George D. Voss, Industrial wood energy conversion, in Fuels From Renewable Resources (D. A. Tillman, K. V. Sarkanen, and L. L. Anderson, eds.) New York: Academic Press, 1977.

12. G. Ray Smithson, Jr., Utilization of energy from organic wastes through fluidized-bed combustion, in Fuels From Waste (L. L. Anderson and D. A. Tillman, eds.). New York: Academic Press, 1977.

13. M. Klar and A. Rule, The Technology of Wood Distillation. London, England: Chapman and Hall, Ltd., 1925.

14. Stanley E. Corder, Wood and Bark as Fuel. Corvallis, Oregon: Oregon State Univ. Forest Research Laboratory, Bulletin No. 14, 1973.

15. The Editors, Discussion of critical issues, in Fuels and Energy From Renewable Resources (D. A. Tillman, K. V. Sarkanen, and L. L. Anderson, eds.). New York: Academic Press, 1977.

16. Paul M. Cheremisinoff and Angelo C. Morresi, Energy from wood waste, Environment 19, No. 4, May, 1977.

17. David A. Tillman, Energy from wastes: An overview of present technologies and programs, *in* Fuels From Waste (L. L. Anderson and D. A. Tillman, eds.). New York: Academic Press, 1977.

18. T. M. Grace, Summary, *in* Forum on Kraft Recovery Alternatives. Appleton, Wisconsin: The Institute of Paper Chemistry, 1976.

19. James A. Knight and M. D. Bowen, Pyrolysis--A Method for Conversion of Forestry Wastes to Useful Fuels. Presented before the Southeastern Technical Division of the American Pulpwood Association, Atlanta, Georgia, Nov. 5-6, 1975.

20. J. A. Knight *et al.*, Pyrolytic Conversion of Agricultural Waste to Fuels. Presented before the American Society of Agricultural Engineers, Stillwater, Okla., June 23-26, 1974.

21. James A. Knight, Pyrolysis of pine sawdust, *in* Thermal Uses and Properties of Carbohydrates and Lignins (Fred Shafizadeh, Kyosti V. Sarkanen, and David A. Tillman, eds.). New York: Academic Press, 1976.

22. J. A. Knight, D. R. Hurst, and L. W. Elston, Wood oil from pyrolysis of pine bark-sawdust mixture, *in* Fuels and Energy From Renewable Resources, D. A. Tillman, K. V. Sarkanen, and L. L. Anderson, eds.). New York: Academic Press, 1977.

23. Personal letter from Dr. Rosely Maria Viegas Assumpcao to Dr. Kyosti V. Sarkanen, Sept. 20, 1977.

24. David L. Brink and Jerome F. Thomas, The pyrolysis-gasification-combustion process: Energy effectiveness using oxygen vs. air with wood fueled systems, *in* Fuels and Energy From Renewable Resources (D. A. Tillman, K. V. Sarkanen, and L. L. Anderson, eds.). New York: Academic Press, 1977.

25. T. B. Reed and R. M. Lerner, Methanol: A versatile fuel
    for immediate use, *in* Energy: Use, Conservation and Supply
    (Philip H. Abelson, ed.). Washington, D.C.: American
    Association for the Advancement of Science, 1974.

26. Gulam Haider, Methanol production from organic waste, *in*
    Fuels From Waste (L. L. Anderson and D. A. Tillman, eds.).
    New York: Academic Press, 1977.

27. CORRIM Committee, The Potential of Lignocellulosic
    Materials for the Production of Chemicals, Fuels, and Energy.
    Washington, D.C.: National Academy of Sciences, 1976.

28. Thomas B. Reed, Efficiencies of methanol production from
    gas, coal, waste or wood, *in* Preprints, Symposium on Net
    Energetics of Integrated Synfuel Systems. Washington, D.C.:
    American Chemical Society, Fuels Division, April, 1976.

29. Kenneth W. Pober and H. Fred Bauer, The nature of pyrolytic
    oil from municipal solid waste, *in* Fuels From Waste
    (L. L. Anderson and D. A. Tillman, eds.). New York:
    Academic Press, 1977.

30. H. R. Appell *et al.,* Conversion of Cellulosic Wastes to
    Oil. Washington, D.C.: U.S. Bureau of Mines Report of
    Investigation 8013, 1975.

31. Irving Wender, Fred W. Steffgin, and Paul Yavorsky, Clean
    liquid and gaseous fuels from organic solid wastes, *in*
    Recycling and Disposal of Solid Wastes (T. F. Yen, ed.).
    Ann Arbor, Michigan: Ann Arbor Science Publishers, 1974.

32. Herbert R. Appell, The production of oil from wood wastes,
    in Fuels From Waste (L. L. Anderson and D. A. Tillman, eds.).
    Academic Press, 1977.

33. Allen L. Hammond, William D. Metz, and Thomas H. Maugh II,
    Energy and the Future. Washington, D.C.: American
    Association for the Advancement of Science, 1973.

34. R. L. Myers and R. L. Miller, St. Regis hydropyrolysis process, *in* Forum on Kraft Recovery Alternatives. Appleton, Wisconsin: The Institute of Paper Chemistry, 1976.

35. G. G. DeHaas, P. J. Hurley, and D. F. Root, Dry pyrolysis approach to chemical recovery, *in* Forum on Kraft Recovery Alternatives. Appleton, Wisconsin: The Institute of Paper Chemistry, 1976.

36. David A. Tillman, The status of coal gasification, Environmental Science and Technology 10, No. 1, Jan., 1976.

37. Bechtel Corporation, Fuels From Municipal Refuse for Utilities: Technology Assessment. Palo Alto, California: Electric Power Research Institute, March, 1975.

38. Frederick T. Varani and John J. Burford, The conversion of feedlot wastes into pipeline gas, *in* Fuels From Waste (L. L. Anderson and D. A. Tillman, eds.). New York: Academic Press, 1977.

39. K. Goddard, Synthetic Liquid Fuels From Coal, Crops, and Waste. Erby, England: Rolls Royce Ltd, 1977.

Chapter 5

THE DEPLOYMENT OF ADVANCED WOOD COMBUSTION AND CONVERSION SYSTEMS

I. INTRODUCTION

Typically wood fuel utilization systems are deployed to
achieve a single purpose such as raising steam. If wood does not
supply sufficient energy for that purpose, the deficit is made
up by those fossil fuels in short supply--oil and gas. In some
plants the problem is too much wood fuel generated by manufacturing processes; and in those cases the solution .employed is to
burn that fuel in less efficient ways [1]. Both of the problems
associated with wood fuels, and the solutions employed, exacer-
bate the nation's long-term energy difficulties. There are
alternative wood utilization systems which help alleviate rather
than aggravate the current national energy situation. These are
advanced deployment systems designed to overcome the inherent
disadvantages of many wood fuels while capitalizing on their
inherent advantages.

There are two advanced deployment systems meriting consideration: (1) co-combustion or co-conversion, and (2) co-generation.
These are depicted, conceptually, in Fig. 1. In the first case,
wood is blended either with coal or with another waste before
energy recovery proceeds. In the second case, wood is used to
generate electricity and process steam or process heat

Cocombustion or coconversion

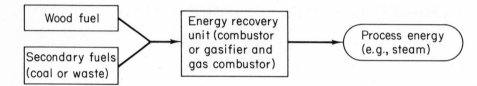

Cogeneration (steam turbine system)

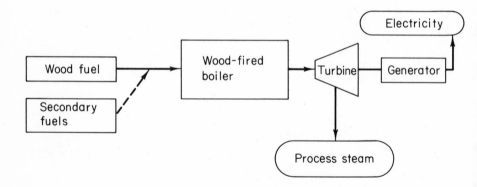

FIGURE 1.   Block diagrams of representative advanced deployment systems for wood fuels.

simultaneously. These advanced deployment systems are not
mutually exclusive; rather, they can be employed simultaneously
if the situation warrants.

II. CO-COMBUSTION AND CO-CONVERSION

Co-combustion and co-conversion address energy supply
issues and aid in the solution of air pollution control problems.
Thus they are of considerable importance in a fuel starved but
environmentally conscious society.

A. *Wood Plus Coal Systems*

The mixing of wood plus coal for combustion purposes permits
a plant to utilize larger combustion equipment and therefore
capitalize upon economies of scale. Further, it permits advancing along the carbon curve as posited in Chapter 3, and leads to
increased combustion efficiencies. In effect, carbon from the
coal partially replaces diluent material in the wood fuel.

The economic advantage of mixing wood fuels with coal
involves capitalizing upon the concept of economies of scale.
Chapter 4 demonstrated that the normal transportation radius for
wood is 30-50 miles. Within a 30 or 50 mile radius the forests
and forest industries produce significant but limited quantities
of fuel. Normally it is posited that wood fuels within a 50-
mile radius could support, at the maximum, a 150 Megawatt power
plant. The optimal sized power plant now, however, exceeds 1000
Megawatts in capacity. Thus for wood fuels to compete in the
marketplace with the more concentrated and transportable fossil
fuels, some blending of wood and coal is highly desirable. Only
in that way can wood participate in fueling the large scale power
plants.

The obvious technical advantages of such mixing have been
known for over 50 years. Hubbard [2] suggests that briquetting

sawdust and coal in a ratio of 5:1 creates a fuel which provides
a higher flame temperature, results in more complete sawdust
combustion, and diminishes the negative influence of moisture by
achieving more rapid water evaporation. Those advantages were
not particularly important in an environmentally neglectful era,
and a time period when oil was beginning to emerge and fuel
resources were apparently limitless. They are important today,
however. Thus co-combustion of wood and coal is being employed
in the forest products industry.

The efficiency and economic considerations are well known.
A third advantage also exists. The inhibition on the use of
coal and, to some extent wood, is air pollution control. The
mixing of these two fuel materials provides a solution to that
problem also. Regarding sulfur oxide emissions, the blending of
wood and coal in a 1:1 ratio (energy content basis) can reduce
<2% sulfur coal to <1% sulfur fuel and permit its use in an
environmentally acceptable manner.

Flick [3] has demonstrated that a more powerful benefit
occurs in the case of particulate emissions when coal is fired
alone or in combination with bark. Fly-ash control is a problem
endemic to both fuels. While wood emits relatively few particulates when compared to coal, they are more difficult to control.
Flick has characterized bark fly-ash as light in weight
(6–15 lb/ft^3), extremely friable, and highly conductive. Thus
it is difficult to control by mechanical or precipitator systems.
Coal fly-ash on the other hand is heavier ($\sim$30–$\sim$50 lb/ft^3), less
friable and less conductive. What appears to be a tradeoff
between fly-ash volume and degree of difficulty in collection is
a synergistic force when the fuels are mixed. Flick observes:
"However, a mixture of bark and coal fly-ash are removed more
effectively than either alone, and very high efficiencies have
been experienced on mixtures up to 50% bark." He points to
particulate emissions (in $lb/10^6$ Btu) of 0.045 using mechanical
collectors combined with either scrubbers or precipitators.

Alternatives exist to co-combustion, including the gasification of coal and wood. Such alternatives provide new options for improved energy recovery and environmental protection, in the latter case by cleaning a smaller volume of gaseous material. In this case, efficiencies can come not only from advancing along the carbon curve but also from using wood as the moisture donor to support the water-gas shift and the steam carbon reactions. This synergy is documented by Rambush, who points out that the additional water required for coal gasification is from 2 to 7 times greater than that required for wood gasification. He further suggests that this steam requirement results in a 7.0% efficiency loss in coal gasification, and only a 2.7% loss in wood gasification [4].

The uses or application advantages of co-conversion as contrasted with efficiency advantages include fuel flexibility. In the forest products industries, there are certain energy applications where gaseous fuels are required (e.g., the lime kiln of an integrated paper mill). Conversion provides the ability to supply those applications as well as the other energy needs of the complex. If wood is used as a fuel outside the forest products industries, this flexibility issue becomes still more important.

Co-conversion has been suggested in numerous pieces of literature. It has been postulated that if modest amounts of wood or waste are combined with coal in a Lurgi reactor, the system would perform adequately [5]. Schulz and coworkers are developing a specific process, the Simplex process, for converting a blend of coal and municipal solid waste (MSW) into synthesis gas [6]. The Simplex process can substitute wood for MSW. This process is now in the early stages of development.

Another approach to this blending process is the mixing of coal and charcoal [7], trading the conversion losses in charcoal production for combustion losses associated with wood fuels. As has been suggested previously, the relative merits of this system are dependent upon the moisture content of the specific wood fuel.

B.   Wood Plus Waste Systems

Wood plus waste (e.g., municipal solid waste, crop waste) systems offer certain obvious economic advantages: (1) increasing the total fuel contribution by biomass in absolute terms, permitting larger scale developments, and (2) providing a mechanism for handling seasonal variations in the volume of waste generated. Again both combustion and conversion systems are available.

The concept of combusting wood and municipal waste is particularly appropriate in wood products areas where communities are likely to be too small to afford the capital intensive resource recovery facilities to make energy from MSW. However, MSW burns well in power boilers if the waste is prepared for such combustion. Groveton Paper Co. in Northumberland, New Hampshire, employs such a co-combustion system and has experienced no particular loss of system efficiency or air quality [8].

The Green Mountain Power Co. Project in Burlington, Vt., is another example of this concept. There a 50 MW power plant is to be fueled with 90% wood waste and 10% municipal solid waste. This project epitomizes the value of combining waste types. Burlington, Vermont, is located a considerable distance away from the production centers of coal and oil. With a population of 38,600, it generates insufficient quantities of MSW to justify a resource recovery facility. And its proximity to wood processing facilities makes wood fuels available. In this case co-combustion provided Vermont its only approach to generating power with indigenous fuels.

A variation on co-combustion is co-conversion of dissimilar wastes into a homegeneous fuel. This can be accomplished by employing the oxygen blown Purox^tm gasifier built by Union Carbide and shown in Fig. 2. In such an approach, synthesis gas ($\sim$350 Btu/ft^3) would be the product. Co-conversion could be performed by air-blown gasification or pyrolysis also. In the pyrolysis case, the Tech-Air system described in Chapter 4 might be used to produce liquid and solid fuels [9]. Co-conversion would be most useful if homogeneous or gaseous fuel is essential to the application.

FIGURE 2. The Union Carbide 200 TPD oxygen blown Purox slagging gasifier unit at So. Charleston, West Virginia. (Photo courtesy of Union Carbide Corp.)

III. CO-GENERATION SYSTEMS

The co-combustion and co-conversion systems can offer modest
incremental gains in efficiency in the case of coal-wood systems,
and economies of scale advantages in all cases. Spectacular
gins can be achieved in energy efficiency, however, if process
heat and electricity are produced from combusting the same fuel.
There are two basic approaches to co-generation: (1) the raising
of industrial steam and heat plus electricity, and (2) the generation of residential and commercial steam for heat plus the
production of electric power. The first concept is normally
called co-generation, while the second is called district heating. It is the first concept which is explored in detail here.

By omitting district heating, this text does not imply that
it is of less importance. The concept is enormously significant.
Karkheck and Powell estimate that over half of the U.S. population could be served by district heating economically. They
estimate that 1×10^9 barrels of oil, or almost 6 quads of
energy, could be saved annually by employing district heating to
its maximum potential [10]. The reason district heating is not
considered further here stems from the fact that wood-fueled
installations, for the most part, are in rural areas where the
district heating potential is limited. District heating logis-
tically is more appropriate for urbanized areas supplied by
fossil fuels. Co-generation, per se, is more appropriate for
wood fuels. Forest products manufacturers are large users of
both process steam and electricity. Thus in the tailoring of a
fuel to its optimum application, wood fuels appear more appropriate to this mode of utilization.

A. *U.S. and European Co-Generation Practices*

Co-generation is not a particularly new idea in this country
or abroad. During the 1920s and 1930s it was exceptionally

popular and profitable in the United States pulp and paper
industry, to such an extent that it caused the U.S. Department
of Justice to institute antitrust proceedings against several
paper companies [11]. Such actions created an institutional bias
against energy efficiency and caused most paper firms to abandon
the practice, at least in terms of outside sales of electricity.
Other barriers to co-generation also emerged. These included
state public utility commission decisions prohibiting electric
utilities from making a profit on electricity generated at plants
other than their facilities (resale electricity); decisions
favoring average rather than marginal pricing for utilities; and
providing utilities with access to lower cost capital through
controlled monopoly provisions [12].

Thus co-generation, as a practice, declined in the U.S. In
1950 it supplied 15% of the nation's energy needs [13], but by
1976, it supplied only 5% of the nation's electricity needs [14].
Only 25% of the total potential application for co-generation in
the U.S. is now being realized [15]. This decline compares somewhat unfavorably with European practice where, for example, West
Germany obtains 30% of its electricity from co-generation.[1] In
Sweden, 50% of the potential for this practice in the pulp and
paper industry is being realized, while in Finland 80% of the
potential in that manufacturing sector is being tapped [15].

Despite legal and institutional problems, co-generation is
again being pursued actively in the U.S. It has become standard
practice on U.S. military bases [16]. It supplies over half of
the pulp and paper industry's electricity needs, 24% of the
chemical industry's needs and 22% of the petroleum and coal
industries' needs [17]. In major segments of the sugar industry,
all electricity comes from co-generation [18]. Companies

---

[1]*These co-generation data include district heating as well
as the generation of process steam and electricity by and for
industry.*

involved in this practice include the St. Regis Paper Co., which
employs co-generation at 12 of its 13 plants [17]; the massive
Dow Chemical Consumers Power complex for generating process steam
for Dow and electricity for Consumers by nuclear power [19]; and
the Gulf States Utilities-Exxon coal-fired project in Beaumont,
Texas, designed to generate 200 megawatts plus $3-4 \times 10^9$ Btu in
the form of process steam every hour [18]. Virtually all fuels
are being employed to accomplish co-generation.

The deployment of co-generation systems based upon wood fuels
is increasing. In Dixville Notch, New Hampshire, the Tillotson
Rubber Co. and the Balsams Hotel resort complex obtain space and
process heat from a wood-fired boiler installation. Electricity
generated from that wood-fired installation is also sold to town
residents. Some district heating is also involved, as excess
steam generated at the co-generation installation is sold to
town residents. The community of Dixville Notch is fueled
entirely with wood. In Oroville, California, Louisiana Pacific
Corporation and Pacific Gas and Electric Co. have planned a
co-generation facility to supply electricity and steam to
Louisiana Pacific's lumber mill and electricity to the utility.
PG&E is committed to developing significant co-generation capability throughout its service area [20].

Other examples of co-generation activity include the planned
coal-fired unit in Geismar, Louisiana, to serve BASF Wyandotte
Corp., Vulcan Materials Co., the chemical division of Shell Oil
Co., Uniroyal, Inc., and Borden, Inc. This planned facility will
have a capacity of 1.8×10^6 lb high pressure steam plus 50 megawatts of power [21]. A municipal waste-based co-generation unit
is planned for Beverly, Massachusetts. This facility will generate 83×10^6 kilowatt/yr for The New England Power Pool, United
Shoe Manufacturing Corp., and The Tyden Group, Inc. It will also
produce 500×10^6 lb steam/yr for those firms plus a local
hospital [22]. A survey run by <u>Area Development</u> Magazine of
those manufacturing companies most concerned with energy showed

that over 25% of the firms polled are contemplating co-generation
systems. Among the larger firms, most reported that they were
"seriously considering" such systems.

B. *The Potential for Co-Generation With Wood Fuels*

The pulp and paper industry not only generates over half of
its electricity needs, but it also sells a modest amount of
power, equal to $\sim 19 \times 10^{12}$ Btu in 1976 [23]. This is no small
accomplishment in a legal climate seemingly designed to ensure
energy inefficiency.

Despite this accomplishment, however, the forest products
industries can make much more use of co-generation than they do
at present. Johanson and Sarkanen estimate that co-generation
could turn the paper industry into a net seller of electricity
rather than a net purchaser of power [15]. The Center for
Environmental Studies at Princeton University estimates that
through co-generation with steam turbine systems, the paper
industry could produce 110% of its electricity needs. With gas-
turbine systems, the paper industry could produce 390% of its
own electricity needs, having available for export nearly three
times the electricity it consumes [17].

C. *Systems Available for Co-Generation*

Two basic approaches exist for gaining this additional energy
supply: the steam turbine cycle and the gas turbine cycle. The
steam turbine system is depicted in Fig. 1. Hogged fuel is combusted for the purpose of raising high pressure steam. This
steam enters an extraction turbine at about 850 psig and 900°F.
After passing through the turbine, it is used for process steam
at 50-150 psig [24]. The process steam is used not only in the
manufacturing activities, but also to heat incoming water. At
such conditions, Gyftopoulos estimates that a 31% relative energy
efficiency increase can be achieved in nonintegrated mills, and a

41% relative energy efficiency increase can be achieved in integrated paper mills, over the efficiency of generating electricity
alone.   The difference of 10% comes from increased turbine efficiencies in larger (e.g., >25 MW) units [24].

In the conceptual gas turbine scheme, wood fuels would be
gasified by one of the technologies described in Chapter 4.
After cleaning and compression where necessary, the gas would be
combusted in a gas turbine with the exhaust heat being used to
raise process steam.   Considerable savings could be obtained by
the increased electricity generating efficiencies of gas turbines
over steam turbines.   Johansen and Sarkanen [15] suggest additional energy plant efficiencies of scale can be achieved by
diverting part of the oxygen used for gasification to the pulp
bleaching operations, and by channeling a portion of the gas produced to the lime kiln, rather than using it to generate electricity.   This permits maximum economies of scale in the design
and installation of all co-generation components.

D. *The Deployment of Co-Generation Systems*

Dow Chemical Co. and Thermo Electron Corp. have both posited
minimum industry requirements in order to make co-generation
economically attractive: the practicality of a generating
capacity of 1-2 MW, and preferably 25 MW; and the operation of
at least 2 shifts/day, 5 days per week, and preferably 3 shifts/
day, 7 days per week [17].   Experience has shown that industries
which consume both electricity and process steam in significant
quantities are the best candidates for co-generation.   Finally,
firms that can own and operate the co-generation system exclu-
sively, rather than being participants in joint ventures, have
better chances of success.   There exist, in such cases, single
or unified investment goals and investment controls.

It has been shown previously that the pulp and paper
industry leads all others in the deployment of co-generation;

and that leadership is expected to continue. The pulp and paper
industry more than fulfills the minimum requirements for
co-generating practicality of 1-2 MW generating capacity and
2-shift operations; most plants fulfill the more preferable
conditions of 25 MW capacity and 3-shift, 7 days per week operations [17]. Additionally the pulp and paper industry requires
large quantities of both process steam and electricity. For sul-
fate pulping, 50-100 kwh and 3-3.5 × 10^6 Btu in other forms,
principally steam, are required to produce a ton of pulp. For
sulfite pulping the requirements are 50-100 kwh and 4-5 × 10^6
Btu. The paper machine requires 300-400 kwh and 5-9 × 10^6 Btu
per ton of product [24].

The pulp and paper industry, because of its internal needs,
can control investment timing by being its major market for both
energy forms. This investment control is critical to the success
of co-generation, as costly delays in joint ventures have documented. The pulp and paper industry has an added advantage, the
use of nonpremium fuel. Only in the Pacific Northwest, where
electricity is incredibly inexpensive, is co-generation
constrained.

That the paper industry will continue to lead in the installation of co-generation systems does not imply that they will
automatically jump into the more capital intensive gas turbine
systems. Gyflopoulos suggests that the lower grade fuel using
industries will favor the steam turbine systems [25]. This is
related not only to the fuel value, but also to the quality of
process steam required [25]. Another force favoring the steam
turbine approach is the overall lack of integration in the forest
products industry where, by and large, lumber mills, plywood
manufacturing plants, and paper mills are not brought together
into a cohesive and coordinated complex. Such a lack of integration impinges upon the efficiency with which capital can be

utilized, hence it favors the somewhat less capital intensive
turbine systems.

The degree of integration in forest products production will
change as raw material and other economic pressures dictate such
integration. Over time, Glesinger's prophecy will become
reality. In 1949 he wrote:

"The thousands of gasoline-powered 'pecker wood' sawmills that
scatter wood waste across the landscape, and the big lumber,
veneer, and pulp mills that stand in distant isolation from one
another, each monopolyzing its own forest dominion, must give way
to integrated forest-industry centers in which all technologies,
old and new, are represented" [26].

This level of integration is developing slowly, as we shall
see in Chapters 6 and 7. In unified production situations, the
gas turbine system makes eminent sense. The Johanson-Sarkanen
system includes gasification of wood plus municipal and agricultural residues and coal when necessary. As Fig. 3 shows, it provides electricity for structural wood plus pulp and paper
operations, oxygen where needed, and gaseous fuel where required.
Such a complex can produce lumber, pulp, paper, and power for
outside sale. It is an optimization scheme for all resources,
not just energy resources.

It is doubtful that additional co-generation will be
deployed in the forest industries using fuels other than wood or
possibly coal. The widely publicized Flambeau Paper Co. situation of 1976-1977, when paper production was severely curtailed,
will discourage co-generation with oil and gas. Flambeau and the
Lake Superior District Power Co. were involved in a co-generation
system fueled by natural gas in Park Falls, Wisconsin. By
October, 1976, gas supplies were lost despite the inherent advantage of the system, as the gas received a low utility rating in
the priority system [27]. This experience did not give
co-generation a black eye, but it did suggest the need for fuel

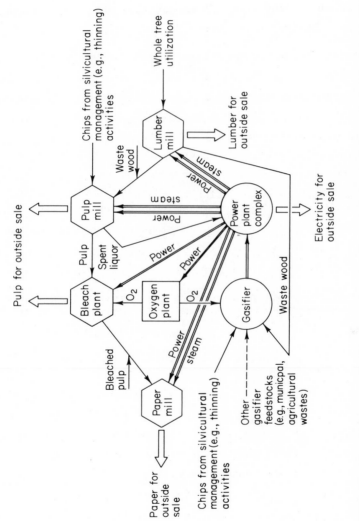

FIGURE 3. The Johanson-Sarkanen concept of an integrated forest products complex employing co-generation.

self-sufficiency in the forest industries, hence the prudence of
using wood fuels. It also illustrated why one-company investment
control is the preferred system.

IV. THE IMPACT OF ADVANCED DEPLOYMENT SYSTEMS

    Advanced deployment systems increase the energy effectiveness
of wood fuels and make them more competitive with the fossil
fuels. Co-combustion and co-conversion of wood plus coal have
both energy efficiency and environmental benefits. Co-combustion
and co-conversion of wood plus waste substitute energy investment
efficiency for energy efficiency, while obtaining synergistic
environmental benefits. Co-generation, which can be performed
with any fuel or combination of fuels, provides the most spectacular fuel efficiency gains of all.

    Table I plots the total supply-delivery trajectories for the
normal wood utilization system, the co-conversion system, and the
co-generation system. This table documents the value of advanced
deployment system, particularly co-generation, for users of wood
fuels. In the co-generation case, the total trajectory energy
efficiency is raised to the $\sim$80% level. Fig. 4 compares the
normal and co-generation wood trajectories, graphically depict-
ing the gains possible.

    In increasing the energy efficiency and flexibility of wood
fuels, advanced deployment systems have the potential for making
the wood products industries virtually energy self-sufficient,
a not insignificant goal for individual corporations and for the
nation as a whole. Johanson and Sarkanen suggest that 0.75 quads
could be contributed, additionally, to the rest of the economy
by using the most advanced deployment system available [16]. In
short, co-combustion, co-conversion, and co-generation will
improve the competitive position of wood fuels. Hence these

TABLE I

Supply-Delivery Trajectories for Wood Fuel Employing Traditional
Deployment Plus Co-Conversion and Co-Generation at 50-Mile Radius
(Assumes harvesting 1×10^{12} Btu for Use)

Energy loss parameter (10^9 Btu)	Wood		
	Normal energy systems	Co-conversion[a] with coal	Co-generation[b]
Energy cost of extraction	25	25	25
Energy cost of transportation	22	22	22
Energy cost of energy recovery	300	280	150
Net energy delivered	653	673	803
Net energy efficiency (%)	65.3	67.3	80.3

[a] Assumes a conversion efficiency of 80%.

[b] Assumes the steam turbine co-generation system with a total
energy recovery efficiency of 85%. This is somewhat lower than
the maximum of 88-89% quoted earlier to reflect conservative
estimates of commercial practice.

systems can, at least initially, accelerate the use of forest
fuels. In the process, reliance on scarce fuels can be moderated.

The National Energy Plan, in two of its less controversial
programs, provides for tax incentives to companies investing in
systems to burn municipal, agricultural, and wood fuels. Additionally it provides incentives for co-generation and promises
the removal of institutional barriers to co-generation [14].
These provisions place the wood fuels in general, and the forest
products industries in particular, in a strong position. These
industries are already moving toward energy self-sufficiency.

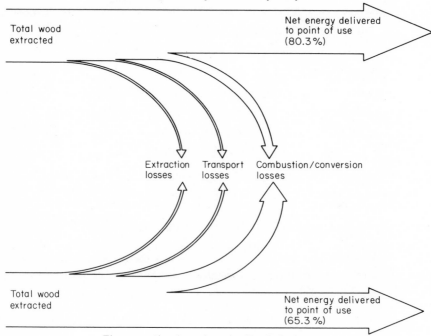

FIGURE 4.   A comparison of co-generation and optimized
conventional wood fuel utilization systems.

Tax incentives plus the more important removal of institutional barriers imposed during an era of apparent energy abundance can only spur that development.

REFERENCES

1. George Voss, Industrial wood energy conversion, *in* Fuels
    and Energy From Renewable Resources (D. A. Tillman,
    K. V. Sarkanen, and L. L. Anderson, eds.). New York:
    Academic Press, 1977.

2. E. Hubbard, The Utilization of Wood-Waste. London,
    England: Scott, Greenwood, 1920.

3. R. A. Flick, Pulping industry experience with control of
    flue gas emissions from bark and wood fired boilers, *in*
    Energy and the Wood Products Industry (Proc.) Madison,
    Wisconsin: The Forest Products Research Society, 1976.

4. N. E. Rambush, Modern Gas Producers. New York: Van
    Nostrand, 1922.

5. K. V. Sarkanen and D. A. Tillman, Concluding discussion of
    salient issues, *in* Thermal Uses and Properties of Carbohy-
    drates and Lignins (Fred Shafizadeh, Kyosti V. Sarkanen,
    and David A. Tillman, eds.). New York: Academic Press,
    1976.

6. Helmut W. Schulz, Energy From Coal and Municipal Solid
    Waste: The Simplex Process for the Production of Synthesis
    Gas. New York: Columbia Univ., 1976.

7. Eugene W. White, Wood charcoal as extender or alternative
    for coal: An immediately available new energy source.
    University Park, Pennsylvania: Pennsylvania State Univ.,
    January 21, 1976.

8. New Hampshire paper mill utilizes nearby town's refuse,
    Catalyst 5, No. 3, 1976.

9. David A. Tillman, Mixing urban waste and wood waste for
    gasification in a Purox reactor, *in* Thermal Uses and Proper-
    ties of Carbohydrates and Lignins (Fred Shafizadeh, Kyosti V.
    Sarkanen, and David A. Tillman, eds.). New York: Academic
    Press, 1976.

10. J. Karkheck and J. Powell, Prospects for the Utilization of
    Waste Heat in Large Scale District Heating Systems. Upton,
    New York: Brookhaven National Laboratory, 1977.

11. Charles A. Berg, Conservation in industry, *in* Energy: Use,
    Conservation and Supply (Philip H. Abelson, ed.). Washing-
    ton, D.C.: American Association for the Advancement of
    Science, 1974.

12. Office of Technology Assessment, U.S. Congress, Analyses
    of the Proposed National Energy Plan. Washington, D.C.:
    USGPO, August, 1977.

13. Executive Office of the President, The National Energy Plan.
    Washington, D.C.: USGPO, April, 1977.

14. Spurgeon M. Keeny, Jr. *et al.,* Nuclear Power Issues and
    Choices. Cambridge, Massachusetts: The Ballinger Pub. Co.
    for the Ford Foundation, 1977.

15. L. N. Johanson and K. V. Sarkanen, Prospects for co-genera-
    tion of steam and power in the forest products industry, *in*
    Fuels and Energy From Renewable Resources (David A. Tillman,
    Kyosti V. Sarkanen, and Larry L. Anderson, eds.). New York:
    Academic Press, 1977.

16. Co-generation of heat and electricity: Why Europe is far
    ahead of the U.S., *in* Energy Research Reports 3, No. 3.
    Newton, Massachusetts: Advanced Technology Publications,
    Feb. 7, 1977.

17. Martin Beiser, Co-generation: Users interested, cautious,
    in Energy User News, July 4, 1977.

18. Co-generation sweetening sugar industry power use, *in*
    Energy User News, Mar. 21, 1977.

19. David A. Tillman, Energy conservation—an accelerating "must" in facility planning, *in* Area Development 11, No. 2, Feb., 1976.

20. Tom Murnane, California waste-wood co-generation planned, Energy User News, Jan. 23, 1978.

21. Michael L. Millenson, Chemical firms near decision on Louisiana co-generation unit, Energy User News, Feb. 20, 1978.

22. Scott Minerbrook, 13 towns join Massachusetts co-generation project, Energy User News, Feb. 20, 1978.

23. J. M. Duke and M. J. Fudali, Report on the Pulp and Paper Industry's Changing Fuel Mix. New York: American Paper Institute, Sept., 1976.

24. Elias Gyftopoulos, John B. Dunlay, and Sander E. Nydick, A Study of Improved Fuel Effectiveness in the Iron and Steel and Paper and Pulp Industries. Washington, D.C.: National Science Foundation, March, 1976.

25. Elias P. Gyftopoulos, Lazaros L. Lazaridis, and Thomas F. Widmer, Potential Fuel Effectiveness in Industry. Cambridge, Massachusetts: The Ballinger Pub. Co., for the Ford Foundation, 1974.

26. Egon Glesinger, The Coming Age of Wood. New York: Simon and Schuster, 1949.

27. Gas cuts wound Flambeau output, Energy User News, Oct. 25, 1976.

Chapter 6

THE RESOURCE BASE
FOR WOOD FUEL

I. INTRODUCTION

Central to any projection of future supply is the determination of whether the resource base of a commodity is adequate to
support the uses contemplated for it, including energy supply.
No fuel material, however valuable, has much of a future if it
cannot be supported by a substantial resource base. If that
lesson is not adequately taught by our experience with oil and
gas, the uncertain future of nuclear power due to a constrained
resource base should permanently imprint the concept in our
minds. Resource availability, more than any other factor, is
spurring on the resurgence of coal. And what of wood?

A. *Traditional Fuel Resource Analysis*

Traditionally, fuels are supplied from fossil fuel resources
and techniques exist for estimating the magnitude of the resource
base. In such an estimation, the base is divided into resources
and recoverable reserves, defined as follows:

resources: concentrations of elements in the earth's
crust or under the sea existing in such a form that they may be
extracted and used.

reserves: masses of rock whose extent and grade are known
to a greater or lesser degree and whose physical natures are

such that they may be extracted at a profit within existing technology and price levels [1].

The relationship between resources and reserves is shown
by the McKelvey diagram, Fig. 1.

B. Resource and Reserve Analysis Applied to Wood Fuel

There are two key differences that separate wood from fossil
fuels: (1) the degree of competition for the resource base, and
the products of that resource base, and (2) renewability. With
fuels such as coal there is essentially one end use available:
energy production. In oil and gas, competition from chemical
industries is significant but relatively minor (∿5%). With wood
there is competition for forest lands from urbanization and
agriculture, competition for the forests from wilderness and to
a lesser extent recreation interests, and competition for the
harvested biomass from producers of lumber, plywood, paper, and
specialty chemicals. With fuels such as coal, formation is so
slow that the resource base can be considered essentially finite,
if very large. When coal is extracted from the earth and

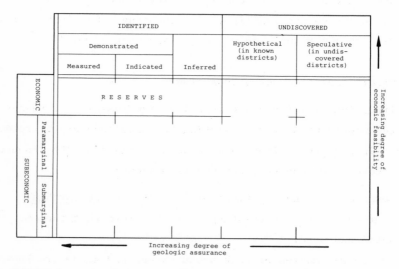

FIGURE 1.   The McKelvey diagram.

used, it is gone. Not so with wood. Wood is renewable. For it
to be extracted and used it must be grown. For wood to be grown,
it must be extracted and used. Like all living objects, trees
pass through a growth stage to maturity, and ultimately to death.
In order to perpetuate growth, harvests must continue in order
to make land available for new trees.

Because of the differences between nonrenewable and renewable
resources, quantifications cannot proceed on comparable bases.
At least in the case of wood fuels, analyses must be broad
assessments of resource adequacy rather than specific point or
confidence interval estimates of resource quantity. Further,
since even the geologic concept *resources* contains no economic
parameters, all analogous estimates of renewable resources are
necessarily more qualitative than quantitative. The analogy
remains valid, however, for it provides a similar starting point
for assessment. Furthermore, it leads to questions of economic
availability, or *reserves,* and then to producibility. By employing a similar starting point, comparable producibility numbers
can emerge, and do emerge in Chapter 7.

C. *Calculating Wood Fuel Resources*

In calculating the adequacy of wood fuel resources, a three-
stage assessment is made. First, the present state of the forest
resource is established. Then competition for products, land,
and forests is assessed. Two types of utilization are considered in this discussion of competition: product and land. As
discussed here, product utilization is the future demand for
fiber to be turned into materials or energy; land utilization
is demand for the forest land from non-forest products interests.
Finally, changes in the renewability are discussed. Such
changes include application of advanced silvicultural methods to
improve the annual biomass production per harvestable acre.

From these discussions, the estimates of the resource base
adequacy are posited.

II.   THE PRESENT WOOD RESOURCE BASE

The total amount of commercial timberland in the United
States has been quite stable over the past few decades, varying
between 495 and 508 million acres [2].   (Commercial timberland,
in this context is defined as land capable of growing 20 ft^3/
acre or 0.3 tons/acre per year or more.)   Table I shows the
distribution of that land by ownership class.

It cannot be assumed from these data that there are ∿500
million acres of commercial forests in the U.S., only that ∿500
million acres potentially could support commercial forestry.
Clearly the 67.3 million acres owned by the forest industry is
being managed for wood production.   Only about 65 million acres
of national forest land has the economic potential for growing
timber [3].   The situation among farm and other private owners
is confusing as some, but far from all, manage their wooded
acres.   Edward P. Cliff, retired Chief of the U.S. Forest Service,

TABLE I

*Area of Commercial Timberland by Type of Ownership in 1952, 1962,
and 1970 (in 10^6 acres) [2]*

Ownership class	Land area		
	1952	*1962*	*1970*
Forest industry	*59.5*	*62.5*	*67.3*
National forest	*93.1*	*94.9*	*91.9*
Farms and other private owners	*296.2*	*306.4*	*296.2*
Other public agencies	*46.2*	*44.4*	*44.2*
Total	*495.0*	*508.2*	*499.6*

has been quoted as saying: "Most of the 296 million acres [of private woodlots] are not poorly managed--they are in effect unmanaged" [4]. While insufficient data exist on ownership objectives, the combination of long lead times for return on investment plus complicated environmental regulations discourages use of this land for timber production [5]. Thus it would be imprudent to plan on a preponderance of this land being used for timber production. Miscellaneous public ownership is another somewhat fragmented category, also experiencing schizophrenia over management objectives. Of the ∿500 million acres of commercial forest land then, it is quite possible that no more than 80%, or 400 million acres, is actually available for forestry purposes.

Within ownership classes, annual land productivity varies markedly. Site classes are used to denote differences in productivity with class I producing >2.5 tons/acre, class II producing 1.8-2.5 tons/acre, class III producing 1.3-1.8 tons/ acre, class IV producing 0.8-1.3 tons/acre, and class V producing 0.3-0.8 tons/acre. Table II shows the distribution of site classes within ownership categories. Clearly the forest

TABLE II

Land Holdings by Site Class (%) [3]

Ownership category	Site class					Total
	I	*II*	*III*	*IV*	*V*	
Forest industry	6	12	28	37	17	100
National forest	3	10	20	38	29	100
Other private forest lands	2	6	25	41	26	100
Other public forest lands	4	8	14	38	36	100
All forest lands	3	8	23	39	27	100

products industry is in a favorable position, and for obvious reasons. Given the amount of land in actual commercial production, this position is essential.

The regional distribution of forest land, based upon the 500 million acre total, shows heavy aggregate concentrations in the east. The highest concentration of most productive land, however, is on the Pacific Coast, as Table III shows. This does not, however, connote that the forest products industry has concentrated its land holdings in the far west. The states with the most forest industry land, in order of absolute size of holdings, are as follows: Maine, Florida, Oregon, Georgia, Washington, Arkansas, Alabama, Texas, Louisiana, and North Carolina [6]. However, wood production is concentrated in the southeast and the northwest.

It is from this land base that timber production comes. The CORRIM Committee [7] and the U.S. Forest Service [2] place annual production for 1970 at 225 million tons of wood and annual consumption at 241 million tons. Table IV provides a distribution of U.S. production and consumption by type of wood. Figure 2 shows the use distribution of that wood harvested,

TABLE III

Productivity of Land by Region (in million acres) [2]

		Region			
Productivity	Total United States	North	South	Rocky Mountains	Pacific Coast
Classes					
I and II	52	10	13	5	24
Class III	116	39	53	8	16
Class IV	196	69	90	14	23
Class V	132	60	36	30	6
All classes	496[a]	178	192	57[a]	69

[a]Not including 5 million "unregulated" acres in Nat. Forests.

TABLE IV

Production and Consumption of Wood (in 10^6 tons including bark) [7]

	Softwood	Hardwood	Total
Production	145.0	79.5	224.6
Import	31.5	6.0	37.5
Export	17.3	3.7	21.0
Consumption	159.2	81.8	241.1
Net import	14.2	2.3	16.5

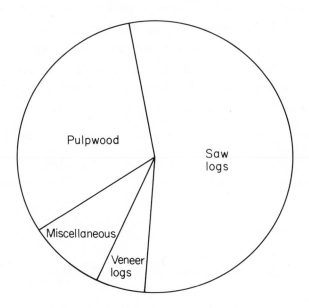

FIGURE 2.   Demand for roundwood by sector [6].

illustrating that at present sawlogs are still the dominant
forest product, although pulp is rapidly achieving parity [8].

Such production can be supported by present forest activities for, As Table V shows, current growth exceeds current use
patterns.   In Table V, only one region shows a growth deficit:
the West Coast.   This anomaly is caused by the preponderance of
old-growth Douglas Fir stands, which exhibit almost no growth at
all.   On harvestable second-growth Douglas Fir stands, growth
does exceed harvest [9].   Thus, as more of the mature West Coast
stands are replaced with new generations of trees, that deficit
could well disappear.

It is clear then, that the forest resource base is more than
adequately supporting the production required of it.   This is
true despite the fact that the tonnage production of wood exceeds
the tonnage production of steel, copper, and aluminum combined.
Is this resource base going to be adequate to support increased
use of wood products in the future, and still supply fuels for
the economy?   To answer that question, we must examine the

TABLE V

Average Annual Growth Per Geographic Area, 1970 (in 10^6 tons) [2]

	Activity		
U.S. region	Growth	Harvest	Ratio growth to removal
North	82.5	36.0	2.3
South	129.0	97.5	1.3
Rocky Mountains	21.0	13.5	1.6
Pacific Coast	46.5	63.0	0.7
Total U.S.	279.0	210.0[a]	1.3

[a]Does not totally agree with Table II due to rounding.

demands that will be placed upon the forest from wood-using
industries and competing interests. Then we can evaluate how
the resource base can be strengthened to meet required demand.

III.   THE DEMANDS PROJECTED FOR THE FOREST RESOURCE BASE

Clawson observes that the economic value of wood production
in the national forest at least equals and probably exceeds the
economic value of wildlife, wilderness preservation, recreation,
watersheds, and all other outputs combined [9]. That statement
is true not only for publicly owned forests, but for all commercial forest lands. Because the forest harvest is far and away
the most valuable output from this resource base, it is essential
to examine the future demand for wood products first, and then
look at other demands that impinge upon our ability to produce
that wood.

A.   *The Demand for Harvested Wood*

Demand projections have been published by the U.S. Forest
Service [2], by Cliff [6], and by the CORRIM Committee of the
National Academy of Sciences [10]. They are virtually identical,
being drawn from the same data base. From these projections it
becomes obvious that demand for harvested wood will increase
significantly by the end of the century and that, in terms of
total tonnages, the demand for wood to be employed by pulp mills
will exceed the demand for lumber. A summary of projections is
presented in Table VI, which demonstrates that, for nonfuel
purposes, roundwood harvests must be raised from 190 to 310
million tons in the year 2000. For materials purposes only, the
wood harvest must increase by 1.64% annually for the remaining
years of this century. At this rate the current wood growth
from the present resource base can support harvests only

TABLE VI

Demand for Roundwood in 1970 and 2000 (in 10^6 tons)[a] [2]

Wood type	1970 Demand	2000 Demand[b]
Saw logs	91.5	114.0
Veneer logs	18.0	30.0
Pulpwood	66.0	153.0
Miscellaneous products	6.0	6.0
Fuelwood	7.5	7.5
Total[c,d]	190.5	310.5

[a] This is demand for roundwood only. Residue consumption is in addition to the above stated totals.

[b] This is the midcase scenario of the U.S. Forest Service, assuming modestly rising prices in real or constant dollars.

[c] Totals do not add in 1970 column due to conversion from ft^3 to tons.

[d] It should be noted that these demand figures assume similar economic relationships to those which existed in 1970. Such relationships could well be changing. If so, demand for pulpwood, for example, or other products could be substantially less than forecast.

until the early 1990s. Entering a temporary wood growth deficit at that time has been forecast by Zivnuska [12].

Such a temporary deficit could emerge sooner if more and more wood is used for fuel or if the resource base is eroded seriously, and the resource base is not improved. In the first case, using the data on energy demand supplied by Grantham [11] and keeping the total growth rate at 1.64%, the deficit could occur in the 1980s, even assuming the same resource base. This situation could be exacerbated by a slow but steady erosion of the resource base.

B. Other Demands for the Forest Resource

Those who would harvest the forest, or some portion of it, are confronted constantly by those who would remove forested lands from wood production. On the one hand, people seeking housing and urban amenities or farmers seeking cropland remove trees from forests and convert the land to other purposes. On the other hand, there are members of society who would preserve more forests essentially intact and prohibit harvesting. Both forces are removing modest amounts of land from harvestable wood production.

The urbanization pressure results from developing housing, shopping centers, roads, rights of way for power lines, sites for industry, and other similar basic needs of a growing population. These results of population expansion annually have consumed 1.2 million acres of commercial forest land in the recent past [8]. There is some evidence that this pressure is abating, for certainly road and airport building have subsided from the peak years of interstate and other transport system construction.

The loss of land to farming, particularly in such areas as the Mississippi flood plain, is more significant. In recent years the net loss has averaged 2 million acres per year. And the lands lost have been among the higher forest site classes [13]. Spurr and Vaux project a net loss, over the next 50 years, of another 20 million acres as a result of agricultural needs [13].

The losses to urbanization and farming may proceed inexorably and, if one assumes a combined loss of 900,000 acres/year, one finds a forest resource base erosion of 27 million acres by the end of this century. At current rates of biomass production, urban and agricultural land needs will reduce commercial productivity by some 15 million tons of wood per year by the end of the twentieth century.

The wilderness and recreation pressures are increasing also.
Such activities can, at times, cripple and constrain wood harvesting. Recreation is a burgeoning industry. Since 1945, the
number of visitors to National Parks has increased from 4.5
million per year to 240 million per year, at a compound annual
growth rate of 15.2% [14]. These visitors have required camping
sites or trails or both and, in the process, have made some portions of the forest lands temporarily or permanently unavailable
for timber production.

This demand for recreation is not expected to moderate in the
ensuing years. Fishman estimates that the demand for camping
areas in National Forests alone will increase by 70% between now
and the end of the century. Based upon a population extrapolation, he has estimated camping use of National Forests--exclusive
of wilderness camping--to rise from 153 million activity days in
1972 to 260 million activity days in the year 2000 [15].
Cicchetti forecasts an increased need for recreation land of up
to 40% [16].

Recreation, per se, need not be a deterrent to timber harvesting. By judiciously applying principles of multiple land use,
both economic interests can be served with essentially the same
resource base. The problem is more with political extensions
of single-purpose interest group arguments. Such political
extensions have led Bethel and Schreuder to conclude that the
U.S. Forest Service is increasingly forced into a custodial role,
managing forests for nonproduction interests. The result is a
vast inventory of publicly owned, overly mature timber [5].

In addition to the demand for the recreation areas in
general, there is a recreation-related specific demand for the
preservation of certain tracts as "wilderness." Some interests
would not only preserve these tracts untouched, but also curtail
cutting on harvestable sites to make them appear more like the
wilderness.

Already, 20 million acres of productive forest land have been withdrawn for recreation and wilderness purposes—effectively removing 11 million tons of annual wood growth from the production system [13]. The wilderness system alone contains 12.3 million acres, although much of it does not come from commercial forests. Currently some 39 million additional acres are either in the proposal or study stages. Spurr and Vaux, assuming that an additional 28.5 million acres will end up as wilderness, forecast that some 9 million acres of commercial forest land will be withdrawn from the productive base for this purpose [13]. At current rates of annual wood growth, this represents the loss of slightly over 5 million tons of production.

The above estimates do not represent the full potential impact of the wilderness-oriented organizations. As was mentioned previously, such organizations periodically attempt to influence the way timber is harvested. Such attempts are designed to preserve the esthetic value of specific tracts of forest land during the time period when harvest-related activities are occurring.

In August of 1975 they obtained a decision from the Fourth Circuit Court of Appeals that the only trees to be harvested in the Monongehela National Forest were those individually marked for extraction. In doing so they reduced the harvest in that forest from 285 million board feet to 30 million board feet, a reduction of 89% [17]. Clearly, broad application of this decision (say to all National Forests) would be disaster. Fortunately the National Forest Management Act of 1976 commuted this threatened death sentence to the wood products industry [18].

Projections presented previously show that, by the end of this century, through actions related to competition for the forest resource, some 20 million tons of annual timber growth will be removed from the productive system. That 20 million tons represents nearly 10% of the present annual harvest, a cut in

the face of a need to increase production by nearly 30% during
the next 22 years. That 10%, which is a modest amount, plus the
30% increase, will have to be made up by changes in renewable
resource management. It is in the area of silvicultural management that the future lies.

IV. RESOURCE RENEWABILITY: INCREASING TREE PRODUCTION
     THROUGH MORE INTENSIVE FORESTRY

The competition for the resource base implies an erosion of
productive timber lands, at least for the remainder of this
century. As has been shown, at current growth rates, that would
be serious. Current rates of forest management will result in
substantially higher, but still inadequate, levels of timber
growth and harvesting. At current rates of management, net
annual growth per acre is expected to rise by 8% by the end of
the century, to >0.62 tons/acre [2]. Even at this rate, only
∿260 million tons of wood would be grown annually in the year
2000, compared to a demand for ∿310 million tons of harvested
roundwood.

The a priori assumptions that current growth rates or current
management rates will continue need not be accepted, however.
Zivnuska makes the obvious point: "Since timber is a crop, the
volume of output can be directly influenced by the level of
inputs devoted to timber growing" [12]. It is only logical to
assume that, over time, those inputs will increase substantially.
Table VII, prepared by the U.S. Forest Service, shows
the significant room for increased productivity, and a significant amount of that improvement could occur in this century.
Obviously, there is a caveat. As the Weyerhauser Co. advertise-
ment points out, the time required to benefit from increased
forest growth is longer than the time required to harvest
carrots.

TABLE VII

Current and Potential Net Growth Per Acre by Ownership Class and Section in ft^3/acre

(tons in parentheses) [2]

Section	1970 and potential	National forest	Other public	Forest industry	Other private	All owner- ships
North	1970	38 (0.57)	33 (0.50)	40 (0.60)	29 (0.44)	31 (0.47)
	Potential	66 (0.99)	59 (0.89)	72 (1.10)	69 (1.05)	68 (1.03)
South	1970	55 (0.83)	45 (0.68)	53 (0.80)	42 (0.63)	45 (0.68)
	Potential	70 (1.07)	71 (1.08)	81 (.122)	80 (1.21)	79 (1.20)
Rocky Mountains	1970	23 (0.36)	23 (0.36)	47 (0.71)	25 (0.38)	24 (0.37)
	Potential	65 (0.98)	54 (0.81)	70 (1.07)	50 (0.75)	61 (0.92)
Pacific Coast[a]	1970	31 (0.47)	63 (0.95)	65 (0.98)	58 (0.88)	49 (0.74)
	Potential	88 (1.32)	100 (1.50)	107 (1.61)	94 (1.41)	99 (1.49)
All sections	1970	30 (0.45)	39 (0.59)	52 (0.79)	36 (0.54)	38 (0.57)
	Potential	76 (1.14)	71 (1.07)	87 (1.31)	74 (1.11)	76 (1.14)

[a]Not including Alaska.

These estimates are somewhat conservative. Techniques
for improving forest growth include (1) site clearing and
immediate reforestation, (2) conversion of hardwood stands to
faster growing softwoods or genetically improved species,
(3) site drainage, (4) fertilization, (5) regular thinning, and
(6) fire, insect, and disease control. Spurr estimates that these
techniques could raise forest wood productivity to 104 ft^3/acre,
or 1.6 tons/acre. Total intensive forest management, he estimates, could raise productivity to 148 ft^3/acre, or 2.2 tons/
acre, annually [17]. The estimate of 76 ft^3/acre is equal
to only 1.14 tons/acre, but even that is double the current output of the forest resource. These numbers include only merchantable wood growth, not total biomass growth. Intensive management
techniques are being utilized increasingly now. Because they
will take on even more significance in the future, they merit
closer scrutiny.

A. *Site Clearing and Immediate Reforestation*

Site clearing and immediate reforestation reduces the time
period when harvested forest lands lie fallow. In reducing the
period of time during which lands are unproductive, crop rotation
times (and hence productivity) can be increased by 3 to 4%.

Replanting of lands has been increased in recent years, after
a decline following the demise of the land bank program. The
acreage reforested during the 10-year period 1962-1971 is defined
by Table VIII. The acreage increased from 1.366 million to
1.667 million in a relatively steady upward trend. Growth came
principally in the forest industry, with modest increases also
in the national forests. Unfortunately the small private owners
and miscellaneous public forests are falling behind, holding
down overall advancement of this practice. Further, as Bethel
and Schreuder suggest, replanting in national forests is not
practiced immediately after harvesting [5]. Despite these

TABLE VIII

Areas Planted and Direct Seeded by Ownership Class for the
Period 1962-1971 (in 10^3 acres) [2]

Year	Ownership class				
	Forest industry	National forest	Other private	Other public	Total
1962	443	198	573	151	1365
1963	467	221	486	151	1325
1964	485	208	460	161	1314
1965	455	233	461	136	1285
1966	475	237	425	144	1281
1967	527	257	457	132	1373
1968	604	269	437	128	1438
1969	681	257	367	127	1432
1970	763	261	422	131	1577
1971	895	267	381	124	1667
Total	5795	2408	4469	1385	14057
Annual Ave.	580	241	447	139	1406

problems, replanting is growing in the forest industry and can
be expected to continue to grow in the future.

B. Conversion of Stands to Faster Growing Species

A method for enhancing the replanting process is to replant
harvested hardwood stands with faster growing softwoods and/or
genetically improved nursery grown species. By converting from
hardwoods to softwoods on some southern pine plantations, rotation times have been reduced to 35-40 years. Figure 3 shows the
nursery growing of conifers at the University of Washington Pack
Forest Nursery. Techniques now exist for rapid genetic improvements of tree species, improvements that will radically shorten

*FIGURE 3.   Growing of trees at the Charles Lathrop Pack
Forest Nursery, University of Washington.*

tree crop rotation times [19].   Weyerhauser Corp., for example,
has given a $1.25 million grant to the University of Oregon to
mass produce trees in the laboratory, trees that will be insect
and disease resistant, and will shorten tree production times by
70-100% [20].

    The results of applying such techniques can be spectacular.
The CORRIM Committee estimates that crop rotations in the south
can be shortened by 20-28 years, to rotation times of 10-12
years.   They estimate that rotation shortening by 10-20 years
from the present ∿60-80 year rotation time can be accomplished
in the Pacific Northwest [10].

C. Site Drainage

A special case in site preparation is site drainage. Some forest lands are too wet to produce at their maximum potential and, in such cases, drainage can improve tree growth. It is not necessary to apply this technique to freshly cleared land, rather, this can be applied to new or existing tree stands.

Drainage in the Scandinavian countries has improve forest productivity by 0.2-0.75 tons/acre annually. While drainage has been inconsequential in the Great Lakes region, it has improved annual productivity by 85% in Loblolly and Slash Pine stands in North Carolina, and it improved Slash Pine productivity by 33% when applied in Florida [7].

D. Fertilization

Like drainage, fertilization can be applied to fresh sites or existing timber stands. Its results are quite significant. Thus, in the last decade, some 900,000 acres of Pacific Northwest Fir stands have been fertilized along with 400,000 acres of southeastern pine stands. Fertilization has been shown to increase annually productivity by as much as 0.7 tons/acre in the four years immediately after fertilization. On average Douglas Fir sites, productivity gains are in the 15-20% range [7,22].

The CORRIM Committee has demonstrated that the most substantial benefit of fertilization is raising the productivity of lower class sites [7]. They have projected the impact of fertilization on Spruce and Redwood lands of the west, and Southern Pine lands of the southeast. The results (Table IX) show decreases in site V lands by 50% or more, and significant increases in site III and site II lands [7]. Because of its obvious benefits, fertilization is being applied increasingly.

TABLE IX

The Impact of Fertilization on Land Productivity [7]

Species and site class	Acreage (in 10^6 acres)		Assumed mean annual growth/ acre (tons/acre/year)
	Before fertili- zation	After fertili- zation	
Spruce, Redwood			
I and II	13.7	15.0	2.2
III	6.5	8.0	1.5
IV	8.2	6.0	1.0
V	1.2	0.6	0.5
Total	29.6	29.6	∿1.3
Southern Pine			
I and II	5.8	6.0	2.2
III	21.9	23.0	1.5
IV	32.0	35.0	1.0
V	8.3	4.0	0.5
Total	68.0	68.0	∿1.3

E.   Thinning

While thinning is probably the most expensive technique for productivity improvement, it also promises the most substantial immediate gains. Further, the material removed by such processes as early thinning (e.g., tree age, 25 years) can be used for such purposes as energy production. Material removed by thinning after age 30 is marketable to many forest industries today. Weyerhauser Corp. predicts a 25% annual increase in Douglas Fir growth by thinning, a prediction supported by research conducted by Spurr, Gingrich, and Andrulot [7].

Thinning has the effect of concentrating soil nutrients in
the most promising trees by removing competition for the
nutrients which can come from the less desirable trees. Because
thinning is productive, 1.43 million acres were so treated
between 1968 and 1970. Trees removed included dead cull
trees and less desirable precommercial growing stock. Acres
treated, by ownership type, were as follows: forest industry
lands, 0.58 million; farms and miscellaneous private lands,
0.42 million; National Forest, 0.33 million; and other public
forests, 0.12 million acres (does not equal sum due to rounding)
[6].

F. *Protection of Existing Stands*

Storms and fires, diseases, and insects are to forest populations what war, famine, and pestilence are to human populations.
Annually they take a fearful toll of trees in the U.S. forests.
Their death toll is now consuming 67.5 million tons of wood,
equal to 20% of the current growth. In 1970, a total of $321
million was spent to control these agents of destruction. If
this level of management is maintained but not increased,
destruction will rise to 78 million tons of wood by the year
2000. With increased expenditures, however, annual losses can
be cut to between 50 and 55 million tons [2]. Such protection
would provide for an increase in harvestible timber of some 20
million tons by the year 2000.

G. *Combined Impacts*

The U.S. forest resource base has been made increasingly
productive, as Table X shows. Since 1952, overall growth per
acre has increased by 30%. While the percentage change indicates
that the largest gains have come on public lands, the absolute
gains in the forest industry are most impressive. There is no

TABLE X

Productivity of Forest Lands in Annual Growth/Acre (in tons)[21]

Ownership	Year			1952-1970 change (%)
	1952	1962	1970	
Total	0.44	0.51	0.57	30
Public	0.36	0.42	0.48	33
Farms and misc.	0.41	0.46	0.54	32
Forest industries	0.64	0.74	0.78	22
North	0.50	0.59	0.61	22
South	0.67	0.78	0.80	19
West	0.73	0.83	0.93	27

reason to believe that these gains will not continue, and at an accelerating pace.

Spurr and Vaux conclude that site improvements, including drainage and fertilization, can increase annual productivity by 1.5%, conversion of forest type can improve growth by 3%, use of genetically improved species can yield a 7.5% gain, and weeding and thinning can improve forest growth by 25%. By the year 2000, the amount of wood available for harvest can be substantially higher than it is today [13]. As an example of this increased productivity, Spurr estimates that Douglas Fir annual growth will go from 0.72 to 1.3 tons per acre as old-growth forests are replaced by faster growing second-growth stands [17].

V. CONCLUSION

Can the forest resource sustain materials and energy production in ensuing years? The answer has to be a qualified yes. While the land base will shrink somewhat, the U.S. Forest Service projects increases of 5% in land ownership by forest industry owners by the year 2000 [2]. Furthermore, the Forest Service reports that toal forestry research expenditures have risen from $86 million in 1960 to $242 million in 1971 [2]. This research should be convertible into productivity gains over the next 30 years.

If this productivity is to emerge from the modestly reduced land base, the forest industries cannot carry the entire burden of increased productivity. At a minimum, the national forests will have to become more productive, meeting demands for timber as well as recreation and wilderness. In all probability, smaller private owners will have to become increasingly involved as well.

There is ample precedent in recent studies for making the national forests more productive. The President's Advisory Panel on Timber and the Environment has recommended that the allowable timber cut in the national forests be increased dramatically [23]. In addition, it recommended specifically: "The commercial forest lands not withdrawn for wilderness or other specific uses should be designated for commercial timber production and other compatible uses and be managed in accordance with appropriate national policies." Among the specific productivity measures recommended by that panel was immediately restocking of harvested lands. In another major study the Comptroller General recommended that Congress appropriate moneys for restocking of 4.8 million acres of national forest, and for completing timber stand improvements (principally thinning) on 13.4 million acres [24].

There is equally substantial evidence that improvements must be made on private lands, particularly those held outside the forest industry. The soil bank program demonstrated that, with some effort, these owners can be reached. Cliff considers their involvement central to the future of forest production [6].

The involvement of national forests and private owners in improved productivity is therefore the caveat. It is the

qualification in the affirmation that U.S. forests can deliver
the materials necessary for materials and energy production.
Clawson, making similar assumptions, has estimated both the
biological and economic potential of the national forests for
the next 50 years [25]. His economic potential estimates show
annual productivity increases of 1.7-2.0% [24]. On this basis,
annual growth in the year 2000 could be 67.5 million tons, or
nearly 25% of the materials requirement. That would be a significant step in the right direction. Assuming other sectors
achieved this 73% gain in productivity by the end of the century,
there would be some 340-350 million tons of wood potentially
available for materials and energy.

Vaux estimates that growth will exceed 400 million tons in
the year 2000 if 1.5 million acres are reforested annually; if
thinning is performed to extract an amount equivalent to 25% of
mortality losses (currently 16.8 million tons), and if annual
investments in planting and road construction are expanded by
$484 million until 1980, by $358 million between 1980 and 1990,
and by $158 million from 1990 until the end of the century [26].
Annual harvests of 340 million tons are estimated by Vaux for
that year, and such harvests can be supported amply with room for
energy production assuming these increases in forest management
intensity [26]. Vaux estimates an additional 20 million tons of
growth in the year 2000 under still more intensive management.

The conclusion, then, is obvious. The forest resource base
can supply the goods and services demanded from it, and can supply energy fuels. Despite competition for the harvested material
and for the land base, improved renewability can provide the
necessary materials. Because this production capability is
demonstrated, it is now essential to determine what forest
resources can be allocated specifically to energy supply. We
shall discuss this in Chapter 7.

REFERENCES

1. John J. Schanz, Jr. <u>Resource Terminology: An Examination of Concepts and Terms and Recommendations for Improvement</u>. Washington, D.C.: Resources for the Future (prepared for the Electric Power Research Institute), Aug. 1975.

2. U.S. Forest Service, <u>The Outlook for Timber in the United States</u>. Washington, D.C.: USGPO, Oct. 1973.

3. Marion Clawson, <u>The Economics of National Forest Management</u>. Washington, D.C.: Resources for the Future, June 1976.

4. The Council on Environmental Quality. <u>Environmental Quality</u> (the Sixth Annual Report). Washington, D.C.: USGPO, Dec. 1975.

5. J. S. Bethel and G. F. Schreuder, Forest resources: An overview, <u>Science</u>, Feb. 20, 1976.

6. Edward P. Cliff. <u>Timber: The Renewable Material</u>. Washington, D.C.: USGPO (for the National Commission on Materials Policy), Aug. 1973.

7. Committee on Renewable Resources for Industrial Materials. <u>Biological Productivity of Renewable Resources Used as Industrial Materials</u>. Washington, D.C.: Nat. Acad. of Sci., 1976.

8. National Commission on Materials Policy, <u>Material Needs and the Environment Today and Tomorrow</u>. Washington, D.C.: USGPO, 1973.

9. Marion Clawson, <u>Forests for Whom and for What</u>. Baltimore, Maryland: Johns Hopkins Univ. Press (for Resources for the Future, Inc.), 1975.

10. CORRIM Committee, <u>Renewable Resources as Industrial Materials</u>. Washington, D.C.: Nat. Acad. of Sci., 1976.

11. John B. Grantham, Anticipated competition for available wood fuels in the United States, *in* Fuels and Energy From Renewable Resources, (David A. Tillman, Kyosti V. Sarkanen, and Larry L. Anderson, eds.). New York: Academic Press, 1977.

12. John A. Zivnuska, U.S. Timber Resources in a World Economy. Washington, D.C.: Resources for the Future, 1967.

13. Stephen H. Spurr and Henry J. Vaux, Timber: Biological and Economic Potential, Science 191, Feb. 20, 1976.

14. America 200: The Legacy of Our Lands. Washington, D.C.: U.S. Dept. of the Interior, 1976.

15. Leonard Fishman, Future demand for U.S. forest resources, *in* Forest Policy for the Future: Conflict, Compromise, Consensus (Marion Clawson, ed.). Washington, D.C.: Resources for the Future, June, 1974.

16. Charles J. Cicchetti, Outdoor recreation and congestion in the United States, *in* Population, Resources and the Environment (Ronald G. Ridker, ed.). Washington, D.C.: U.S. Commission on Population Growth and the American Future, 1972.

17. Stephen H. Spurr, American Forest Policy in Development. Seattle, Washington: Univ. of Washington Press, 1976.

18. Monongehela Controversy Resolved by Law, Wood and Wood Products. Chicago, Illinois: Vance Publishing, Dec. 1976.

19. Claud L. Brown, Forests as energy sources in the year 2000: What man can imagine, man can do, J of Forestry 74 (1), Jan. 1976.

20. Monte Mace, Test tube babies, Wood and Wood Products J 81 (9), Sept. 1976.

21. Harbridge House, Spot shortage conditions in 1973-1974: The pulp and paper industry experience, *in* The Commodity Shortages of 1973-1974: Case Studies. Washington, D.C.: USGPO, Aug. 1976.

22. Regional Forest Nutrition Research Project. Seattle,
     Washington: Univ. of Washington, 1977.
23. Report of the President's Advisory Panel on Timber and
     the Environment. Washington, D.C.: USGPO, April 1973.
24. The Comptroller General, More Intensive Reforestation and
     Timber Stand Improvement Could Help Meet Timber Demands.
     Washington, D.C.: General Accounting Office, Feb. 1974.
25. Marion Clawson, Man, Land, and the Forest Environment.
     Seattle, Washington: Univ. of Washington Press, 1977.
26. H. J. Vaux, Timber resource prospects, in Timber!
     (William A. Duerr, ed.). Ames, Iowa: Iowa State Univ.
     Press, 1973.

Chapter 7

THE POTENTIAL SUPPLIES
OF WOOD FUEL

I. INTRODUCTION

While the wood resource base can be made adequate to meet
the myriad of demands put on it, specifically what portion of
that resource base will be available for supplying wood fuels?
Will residues continue to supply the necessary energy materials
for the boilers and kilns of wood fuel using industries? Will
tracts of land be set aside for growing wood fuels? Answers to
these questions provide a basis for estimating the quantity of
wood fuel available for use. In doing so, such answers offer a
means for estimating wood fuel *reserves*, that portion of the
resource base that can be recovered for energy purposes within
the framework of current technology and price levels.[1]

To apply the concept of reserves with some degree of confidence, certain parameters must be established. For purposes of
this discussion, the harvesting or recovery of wood for energy
purposes is considered economic when the following situations
hold:

---

[1] *As with Chapter 6, the aspect of renewability rules out
direct comparison with mineral fuel reserves despite the
validity of applying the concept. It is in producibility that
comparability exists.*

(1) when there is no higher value market for the wood materials so recovered; and

(2) when the material, so recovered or produced, can compete economically with alternative fuels.

If one or the other condition fails to exist, then it is not economic to produce energy from that wood material under consideration.

In order to assess the total reserve base for wood fuels, it is essential first to evaluate the questions of residue availability and competition for residues. From there the longer term concept of energy farming can be considered.

II. WOOD RESIDUES AS RESERVES

The question of wood residue availability is more complex than the question of energy farming. Residue availability is a function of several production rates (1) forest growth and growth management, (2) logging or extraction, and (3) primary product (e.g., plywood) production. It is also a function of residue utilization rates (e.g., the use of sawmill residues by the pulp and paper industry). One can employ the following conceptual formula to calculate annual residue available for energy purposes:

$$R_E = \Sigma (R_G - R_U) - R_M$$

where R_E is residues available for energy; R_G is residues[2] generated by (a) forest growth and mortality, (b) forest management practices, (c) forest harvesting practices, and forest products manufacturing processes; R_U is residues that

---

[2] *Residues generated by building demolition, wood products discard, and other similar activities are treated as urban residues and not considered in this discussion.*

are uneconomic to collect and use; R_M is residues used for
materials production including (a) pulp and paper, (b) particleboard and other composition boards, (c) chemicals, and (d) agricultural products (e.g., mulch, cattle feed).

After gross availability has been calculated, economic availability can be assessed considering net alternative costs of
treating such residues. For example, if it costs more to
recover logging residues for energy than to purchase available
alternative fuels, then logging residues are not economically
available.

A. *Wood Residue Generation*

Wood residues of forest growth and management, forest harvesting, and wood products manufacturing have all been calculated
for present practices. Making certain assumptions consistent
with the data found in Chapter 6, they can be projected to the
year 2000.

1. *Residues of Forest Growth and Management.* As was
pointed out in Chapter 6, trees like all living organisms go
through various cycles including rapid growth, maturity, and
death. At present, death comes to 4.5 billion ft^3 of growing
stock (equal to 67.5 million tons of wood) annually [1]. This
material is killed by insects, fire, and other natural causes.
The accumulation of this material, plus unusable trees, is now
in the vicinity of 1 billion tons, as Table I shows. Some 20
million tons of this material is cut annually by logging
operations and left with logging residues.

One notable case of dead trees available for energy conversion is in Maine, There, some 7 million acres of fir trees
have been infested with spruce budworm. Within two years of
infestation, these trees are unusable for producing lumber or
paper; yet, in the woods, they are a serious fire hazard. The
last such spruce budworm infestation in Maine destroyed

TABLE I

Availability of Noncommercial Timber (in 10^6 oven dry tons) [2]

Region	Rough trees	Rotten trees	Salvable dead trees	Total
North	165.6	111.9	3.7	281.2
South	265.8	106.1	3.4	375.3
Rocky Mountains	37.8	41.9	100.5	180.2
Pacific Coast	39.6	35.7	72.9	148.2
Total	508.0	295.7	180.5	984.9

65 million cords, or ∿160 million dry tons of wood, and the present infestation is considered worse [3]. These wasted tons of trees are not fully reflected in Table I, since the data base for that table was developed in 1970, before the rampant spreading of the spruce budworm plague.

The annual accumulation of dead trees, if forest management activities do not exceed present levels, is expected to rise to 4.9 billion ft^3 or 73.5 million tons in 1985, and to 5.2 billion ft^3 or 78.0 million tons in the year 2000 [1]. If management levels increase, however, production of such residues can be reduced to about 3.5 billion ft^3 or 55 million tons annually.

As in the state of Maine, most of this material is permitted to remain in the woods. Its removal would not only reduce the hazards of conflagration and pestilence, but would also stimulate more rapid growth of the remaining healthy trees. Further, its removal would increase the scenic and recreation values of the forest [2].

Natural forest processes produce worthless biomass other than dead trees. Forest cutting or forest fire followed by natural regeneration can produce low-value stands of mixed hardwoods, stands that must be removed if productive forestry is to be practiced. These mixed hardwoods are not traditionally

defined as residues, yet they are valueless biomass materials
that impede sound silviculture. Thus they are included here.
In the south, some 30 million acres of mixed oak and pine forests
exist, along with 88 million acres of slow-growing hardwoods [4].
Other regions have similar situations. In the intensified
management described in Chapter 6, significant amounts of these
materials would be removed and be made available for energy purposes.

Intensified forest management produces still another type of
residue: thinnings from growing stands. Thinning now occurs,
and is increasing. Unfortunately, precommercial thinnings are
presently left in the woods, where they rot. The production of
timber residues from thinning is expected to increase. Vaux
places the amount at 25% of mortality losses for the remainder
of this century under increasing management intensity [2]. Such
an effort would produce some 14 million tons of wood that could
be used as fuel.

Table I summarizes the production of residual materials by
the forest and forest management practices. As Table II shows,
there is a backlog of 16×10^{15} Btu (or quads of energy, and
the annual production is between 1.1 and 2.0 quads.

2. Residues of Wood Harvesting. Logging residue generation
is a function of the total annual tree harvest plus the rate at
which that residual material is recovered for product utilization. Presently 10-15% of the wood harvested is left in the
forest or burned there, as logging residue [5]. In 1970 this
constituted 1.6 billion ft^3 or 24 million tons of material.[3]

[3]*These numbers do not include the cull material removed during logging operations, treated in the previous section. Further,
the tonnages are based on stem wood. If branches are included,
the number can be approximately twice as large. If leaves and
needles are included, it can be four times as large. Because
there is some question concerning the removal of nutrients from
the forest by harvesting all portions of the tree, the most
conservative number has been used here.*

TABLE II

Summary of Projected Forest and Forest Management Residues
Produced Annually by the Year 2000

Type of residue	Annual production	
	10^6 million	10^{15} Btu
(Backlog of noncommercial timber)	(984+)	(16.0)
Mortality	55	0.9
Conversion of mixed hardwood stands	55^a	0.9^a
Thinnings	14	0.2

^{a}Assumed to be equal to mortality.

If one assumes that the total harvest will rise from the
present level of 199 million tons to 242 million tons in 1985
and 310 million tons in the year 2000, then one can forecast the
generation of 43 and 54 million tons of logging residues, as
currently defined, produced in those two projection years. Such
tonnages are equivalent to 0.68 and 0.88 $\times 10^{15}$ Btu, respectively.[4]
Such residues can be expected to be most available in the South
and on the Pacific Coast, where most timber harvesting occurs.

3. Residues of Forest Products Manufacturing. The production of mill residues represents the most significant generation
of potential wood fuel materials. Again such production rates
are determined by the manufacture of lumber, plywood, veneer,
and paper. Using the production projections of the U.S. Forest
Service [5], one can derive residue generation estimates. These

[4]To put this in perspective, at the height of the oil embargo
of 1973, only 1 million barrels of oil per day, equal to 2 quadrillion Btu/yr, were withheld from the U.S. economy, with nearly
catastrophic results. The Alaska pipeline is designed to deliver
a maximum of 4.8 quadrillion Btu to the economy annually.

are presented in Table III. The projections used were the
medium values, assuming a total demand for 20.7 billion ft^3 of
roundwood in the year 2000. Demand could rise to 22.8 billion
ft^3 (342 million tons) in that year, or fall to 19.2 billion ft^3
(288 million tons). The middle value estimates have an energy
content of 3.2 × 10^{15} Btu.

In summary, then, there is a backlog of 16 × 10^{15} Btu in
forest residues. Additionally, the total annual residue production will rise to 4.5 × 10^{15} Btu in 1985 and 5.2 × 10^{15} Btu in
the year 2000. These residues plus fuel wood harvested form the
base from which wood fuels will be derived.

B. *Wood Residue Availability*

The generation of residues is one component in the equation;
economic availability is yet another issue to be dealt with.
Clearly manufacturing or mill residues, collected and concentrated, can be considered economically available. What of the
forest residues?

If one assumes that the cost of harvesting dead trees and
thinnings by whole tree chipping is no more than twice the normal
harvesting cost,[5] then approximations of forest residue extraction costs can be made. Stanford Research Institute has calculated the costs of harvesting logging residues and delivering
them to a central point for two areas of California and for
Maine. These costs have also been estimated by Grantham [6].
The costs of both practices are presented in Table IV, both in
$/O.D. ton and in $/10^6 Btu. Crude estimates show an average
of $2.25–2.50/10^6 Btu for the extraction of such material.

---

[5]*This is the most expensive form of tree harvesting since
it precludes the use of much mechanized equipment in the actual
extraction. Chippers at landings can be employed, however.*

TABLE III

Wood Consumption and Mill Residue Generation in the U.S. to the Year 2000 (in 10^6 tons) [1]

Product	Year		
	1980	1990	2000
Saw log consumption	93	105.5	114
Residues generated	62	70.6	75.6
Veneer log consumption	24	27	30
Residue generated	13.4	15.1	16.8
Pulpwood consumption	88.5	117.0	153.0
Residues generated			
Bark	3.5	4.7	6.1
Spent liquor solids	57.5	76.1	99.5
Miscellaneous products	6	6	6
Residues generated	1.2	1.2	1.2
Fuelwood	7.5[a]	7.5	7.5
Residues generated	None	None	None
Total wood consumed[b]	219.0	264.0	310.5
Residues generated	137.6	167.7	199.2
Energy equivalent (10^{15} Btu)	2.2	2.7	3.2

[a]This is the U.S. Forest Service projected value which disagrees with the author's estimates, to be presented later.

[b]It should be noted that additional products will be manufactured from residues; residues are not used to decrease the totals of roundwood consumed.

TABLE IV

The Cost of Extracting Forest Residue

Residue type	$/ton	$/10^6 Btu
Forest residues: dead or		
unmerchantable trees, thinnings [8]	20-60	1.25-3.75
Logging residues [8]		
Sutter, California	25-41	1.60-2.60
Humbolt, California	24-44	1.50-2.75
Maine	20-60	1.25-3.75
Logging residues [6]	29.70	1.85

Those prices are gross costs, the benefits of increased growth in the forest from which residues are extracted, or in the case of logging residues, the present costs of waste disposal have not been used to reduce those figures to net costs. Quantification of the benefits is extremely site specific.

Quantification of the costs of logging residue disposal has been performed by Grantham for the Pacific Northwest. These costs, by treatment, are as follows: burning in place, $2.00/ton; yarding and burning, $6.40/ton; and removing to a manufacturing plant material above 4 in. diam., $12.80/ton [6]. The first two costs, if subtracted from the average extraction cost of logging residues, reduce the energy price to about $2.00/10^6 Btu. This is equal to $11.60/bbl of oil.

Yarding unmerchantable material (YUM), the option costing $6.40/O.D. ton, is being required increasingly in the national forests. The YUM practice is expected to increase significantly in the future. Thus one can expect the net costs of removing forest and logging residues to be within the current price range of refined petroleum fuels. Forest residues are somewhat appealing as a future fuel source even now.

One conceptual approach to making forest residue fuels more attractive is in-woods drying and processing. In this approach a portable dryer or pyrolysis unit is taken into the woods to treat hogged logging residues and/or forest management residues. Such a system is powered by forest fuels. Thus the energy cost of upgrading forest residues can be considered to be zero since, otherwise, the branches and other waste would go totally unutilized. The Georgia Tech – Tech Air approach includes one such portable pyrolysis unit which could produce fuel for $\sim$\$2.25/ 10^6 Btu. If such an approach were employed the char could be mixed with the oil for transport and combustion. This complete conversion approach would have to compete, economically, with hogging and drying or hogging and transporting. Figure 1 is a drawing of the portable conversion unit developed by the Georgia Institute of Technology [36].

The economics of wood fuel utilization, when compared to alternative fossil fuels, can be summed up by the following formula:

$$FC = \frac{\$/10^6 \text{ Btu of } NHV}{FE}$$

Where FC is true fuel cost, NHV is net heating value (in 10^6 Btu) per ton, and FE is total fuel efficiency or trajectory efficiency. Forest residues now have a true fuel cost of $\sim$\$3.90/10^6 Btu and, if processed, have a true fuel cost of $\sim$\$3.20/10^6 Btu. This is already very close to the marginal true cost of oil or natural gas. Hence forest residues will be used in the near future. As premium fuel prices rise to \$4/10^6 Btu and above[6] (imported crude oil now costs \$2.40/10^6 Btu landed

---

[6]*Earl T. Hayes has forecast that energy prices will rise to \$4.00/10^6 Btu in 1976 dollar terms by 1985, and the economy will have to adjust to such energy costs [10]. This is still relatively cheap energy. Earl Cook has calculated that labor paid \$3.00/hour costs \$6000/10^6 Btu [11].*

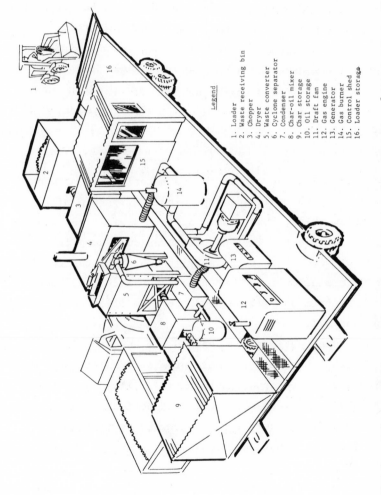

FIGURE 1. Transportable pyrolytic waste conversion system. [(1) Loader, (2) waste receiving bin, (3) chopper, (4) dryer, (5) waste converter, (6) cyclone separator, (7) condenser, (8) char-oil mixer, (9) char storage, (10) oil storage, (11) draft fan, (12) gas engine, (13) generator, (14) gas burner, (15) control shed, (16) loader storage.] Drawing courtesy of Georgia Institute of Technology Engineering Experiment Station.

Legend

1. Loader
2. Waste receiving bin
3. Chopper
4. Dryer
5. Waste converter
6. Cyclone separator
7. Condenser
8. Char-oil mixer
9. Char storage
10. Oil storage
11. Draft fan
12. Gas engine
13. Generator
14. Gas burner
15. Control shed
16. Loader storage

in the U.S.), these residues will be attractive indeed!   Thus,
for 1985 and beyond, virtually all wood residues can be considered to be economically available.

C.   *Competition for and Uses of Those Wood Residues*

    Glesinger lays down the following principle: "No wood that
can serve some other useful purpose should be burned" [9].
Given that statement, it is essential to examine the forecast
demand for wood residues by the manufacturers of pulp, particleboard and other composition board, and chemicals.   What they
will not use can be considered as economically available for
energy production.

    1.   *The Use of Residues in Pulp Production.*   The use of wood
residues as a significant source of raw materials is perhaps
symbolized best by the pulp and paper industry.   Pulp mills
regularly employ chips, shavings, and other sawmill residues as
a basic source of fiber.   In 1960, such residues supplied 6.75
million tons of wood to that industry, and by 1975 the total had
climbed to 28.8 million tons.   Roundwood harvested for pulp
production rose from 33 million cords to 49 million cords during
the same period [7].

    While residues, nationally, assumed the burden of 37% of pulp
fiber supply, they became still more prominent on the west
coast.   Figure 2, taken from Grantham [12], illustrates that the
dramatic expansion of west coast pulp production was predicated
totally upon residue consumption.   Roundwood harvested for
pulping purposes there has declined by 50% over the 20 year
period 1951-1971.

    As one looks to the future, the increased use of residues for
pulp manufacture can be forecast.   Falkehag [13], recasting data
from the Outlook Report of the U.S. Forest Service [5], has
projected the use of 38.2 million tons of wood residues by
paper mills in 1985, and 45.1 million tons in the year 2000.

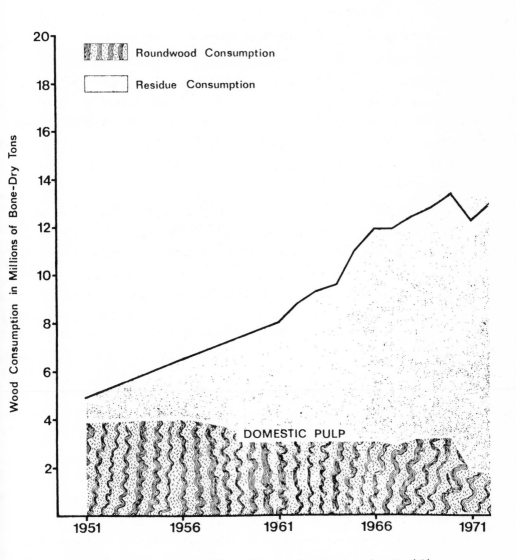

FIGURE 2. Sources of fiber for wood pulp on the Pacific
Coast. Source: [12].

The bulk of this material will be supplied by sawmill residues.
There is little problem in supplying this quantity of mill residue in the year 2000, as the residue generation discussion states.
Although the CORRIM Report [4] suggests that chipping of logging
residues will provide modest amounts of fiber to the pulping
industry, Poyry Engineers [14] point out that grit entrained in
the bark during harvesting, increased chemical consumption, and
decreased fiber yield are among the technical problems limiting
the use of such chips for pulping. Chips containing bark are
not expected to make significant inroads in the near- and mid-
term future.

2. *The Use of Residues in Particleboard and Other Structural Products.* In this age of rediscovering old concepts as
new catch phrases, it is worth remembering that the masonite and
particleboard industries were created specifically to use forest
industry residues. By 1970 the entire family of structural wood
industries consumed 7.5 million tons of residue for product
manufacture. By 1985 that total is expected to rise to 14.4
million tons, and by the year 2000 it will probably rise to 19.6
million tons [13].

Like pulp, particleboard and the other structural wood substitutes will continue to rely upon mill residues rather than
logging residues. Feedstock quality considerations dictate minimum amounts of bark and sawdust in the raw material used, a
specification that limits input materials to coarse mill
residues.

3. *The Use of Residues for Producing Chemicals from Wood.*
Currently wood is supplying some 1.7 million tons of dissolving
pulp for the production of cellulose-based plastics, rayon, and
related chemicals. The regenerated cellulose products are used
to manufacture synthetic textile fibers along with less significant products such as eyeglass frames, automotive parts, and

pharmaceuticals. Regenerated cellulose is employed when quality
considerations override least-cost price issues [4].

In addition to regenerated cellulose, numerous wood-based
chemicals are produced as by-products of the kraft and sulfite
pulping processes and from the gum naval stores industry of the
southeastern United States. The by-products of kraft and sulfite
pulping include such products as lignin sulfonates [15]. Other
products include dimethyl sulfide and tall oil [15,16]. Lignin
products are also essential in the development of "drilling muds"
used in the exploration and extraction wells for petroleum production [16]. Gum naval stores include turpentine used in oil-
based paints plus adhesives, disinfectants, insecticides,
and resin acids [17].

Since the basic raw materials for plastics and chemicals are
petroleum and natural gas, it is often suggested that wood could
be employed as a basic raw material substitute. Bungay and
Ward [18] posit this as one optimum end use of the energy farm.
The CORRIM Report also suggests this possibility. Numerous
authors have gone beyond these general observations, suggesting
the possibility of producing additional specific chemicals.

Goheen and Henderson have presented research performed by
Crown Zellerback suggesting that high-temperature pyrolysis of
lignin can be employed to produce acetylene and other unsaturated hydrocarbons [19]. Acetylene yields of up to 15% have been
achieved in these experiments. They concluded that, theoretic-
ally, yields of 37–40% C_2H_2 were possible and yields of 25% were
reasonable. Minor amounts of ethylene were formed in these
experiments. Goheen has also produced quaiacol experimentally
by high-temperature indirect pyrolysis of spent liquor solids.
Again, significant yields of this chemical were achieved, suggesting that there is promise for producing the high-value
product from wood [20].

Falkehag has reported encouraging results purifying lignin from spent liquor, and employing it as a carbon black substitute. This material can be used as reinforcing for styrene-butadiene rubber (SBR) in such products as rubber tires [13]. The resulting reinforced SBR is virtually identical in quality to that reinforced by carbon black made from traditional sources.

There is a constant theme through these chemical production schemes: the resulting chemicals are of minor economic importance in terms of total volume. The high-volume materials, other than ammonia, include plastics such as polyvinyl chloride (PVC), polystyrene, and polyurethane. All are petroleum and natural gas based.

The reasons why wood is not a likely feedstock for petrochemicals are twofold: (1) wood is composed of natural high polymers, which must be completely broken down and reformed in order to create plastics such as PVC; and (2) the petrochemical industry is moving to maximize the use of oil. In the first case, the processes for reconverting wood into new polymers rarely exceed 30% in efficiency. In the second case, the strengthening of oil use, Union Carbide Corp. and Kureha Chemical Co. have developed a refining process to take crude oil directly to ethylene, propylene, and other basic building blocks of petrochemicals: at between 60% and 80% efficiency [21]. Since this process is an extension of existing technology and promises to stretch available reserves of oil, it offers the opportunity for the chemical industry to remain petroleum based well into the twenty-first century.

At present, the chemical industry consumes 5% of the natural gas and petroleum used in this country. Given the economic disadvantage of wood vis-a-vis oil, it is inconceivable that more than 2% of the residues produced would be used for chemicals manufacture. Thus, only about 7.0 million tons would be used for such purposes in 1985, and at most 7.2 million tons in the year 2000.

   *4. Total Nonfuel Consumption of Wood Residues to the Year
2000.* The consumption of wood residues for nonfuel purposes is
shown in Table V. For all categories of use, it is rising significantly as the forest products industry seeks to maximize
utilization of its harvested material. It is clear that these
uses will continue to increase. Without such residue fiber
availability, the output of the forest products industry would
indeed be constrained.

D. Wood Residue Available for Energy Purposes

   What wood will be available for conversion into fuels and
energy? It will be unused residues plus whatever material is
harvested locally from existing stands as fireplace wood. The
residues can be estimated by the formula posited in Section II.
The firewood harvested is a demand-driven value; thus 20% above
present levels is used here as an expedient upper bound. The
summation of these two values constitutes fuel wood reserves and,
simultaneously, annual fuel wood producibility.

TABLE V

*Consumption of Wood Residues for Nonfuel Purposes to the Year
2000 (in 10^6 tons)*

Industry	1970	1985	2000
Pulp and paper	24.5	38.2	45.1
Structural wood products (e.g., particleboard)	7.5	14.4	19.6
Chemicals	4.0	7.0	7.2
Total	35.0	59.6	71.9
Total (in energy equivalent, 10^{15} Btu)	0.56	0.95	1.15

Table VI summarizes wood fuel producibility to the year 2000. It demonstrates that by the year 2000, 4.5×10^{15} Btu could be produced easily from wood and, with more intensive forest management, some 5.8×10^{15} Btu could be produced (see footnotes to Table VI). Thus numbers are not hard and fast. If one assumes more lumber production, then the result will include more wood fuel production both in harvesting residues and in mill residues. Similar increases could come from forest management programs of a highly accelerated nature. These numbers, then, are moderately conservative estimates of the material likely to be available for conversion into energy.

It is useful to put these numbers into a comparative framework, illustrating how wood fuel producibility compares with other options. Since the assumptions made in this chapter are comparable to the extension of existing conditions or market assumptions of the Committee on Nuclear and Alternative Energy Systems [22], results are also comparable. Table VII presents producibility estimates for selected fuels, including wood, to the year 2000. It can be seen from Table VII that wood and nuclear power can be making equal contributions for the remainder of this century. By the year 2000, taken together, they can more than equal the production of natural gas.[7]

The minor or emerging fuels (solar energy, geothermal power, municipal waste, and agricultural waste) are not shown in Table VII. The data base for forecasting is insufficient at this time, and more experience is needed. Hydroelectric producibility is not shown due to a fundamental disagreement on

---

[7]The contrast, however, is that by the year 2000 we will be short of uranium. As Boyd and Silver have pointed out, our total resource base of U_3O_8 is in the vicinity of 692 quads-- or 175 quads when converted to electricity by light water reactors. Further, it is quite possible that we will not find a significant portion of those resources. Thus, by the year 2000 we could be in worse shape on uranium than we are now on oil and natural gas [23].

TABLE VI

Annual Wood Fuel Producibility to the Year 2000 (in 1 $\times$ 10^{15} Btu)

	1970	1985	2000
Residues produced			
Forest residues	1.00	1.10[a]	1.10[a]
Harvest residues	0.38	0.68	0.88
Mill residues	2.20	2.70	3.20
Total residues produced	3.58	4.48	5.18
Residues used for materials purposes (in 10^{15} Btu equivalents)			
Pulp and paper	0.39	0.61	0.72
Structural products	0.12	0.23	0.31
Chemicals	0.06	0.11	0.12
Total residues used	0.57	0.95	1.15
Total residues available for fuel	3.04	3.53	4.03
Estimated fuelwood harvested	0.20	0.50[b]	0.50
Total wood fuel producibility	3.24	4.03	4.53

[a] *Does not include conversion of mixed hardwood stands to faster growing species, which, if performed, could easily supply 0.5 $\times$ 10^{15} Btu to the economy. Also does not include backlog of 1 billion tons of dead or otherwise unusable timber, which, if extracted at 5% per year, could contribute 0.8 $\times$ 10^{15} Btu annually to the economy.*

[b] *This is 20% higher than 1976 consumption, estimated at 0.4 $\times$ 10^{15} Btu.*

TABLE VII

Producibility of Selected Fuels to the Year 2000 (in 1 × 10^{15} Btu) [22]

Fuel	Producibility		
	1976[a]	1985	2000
Coal	16.2	19.9	34.0
Domestic petroleum	20.0	18.0	12.0
Domestic natural gas	19.7	13.5	7.0
Shale oil[b]	-	0.2	1.0
Nuclear power[c]	1.8	2.3	4.8
Wood[d]	1.6	4.0	4.5

[a]Production.

[b]Adjusted from U_3O_8 production, light water reactors only.

[c]Used enhanced projections to reflect more recent information [24].

[d]The estimates of this author, not CONAES.

how much can be produced. Most existing forecasts show little room for growth; however, some others show surprising potential for increasing this clean, cheap source of energy.

If wood can supply 4.5 to 5.8 × 10^{15} Btu to the economy, then one essential question remains: How much will it supply by the year 2000? The answer to that question will help define the role and position of this combustible renewable resource as we move inexorably into the next century. If we are to use the 4.5 × 10^{15} Btu available, then wood fuel consumption will have to increase 180% in 24 years. That is not impossible, but it is certainly a herculean task. If we are to use less than that, then waste disposal costs will continue to plague us, along with oil import costs. If we are to use more than 5.8 × 10^{15} Btu then wood fuel extraction costs will escalate. Thus matching of producibility and projected consumption estimates

is essential. From this matching the precise definition of
of wood's role as an energy resource can be determined.

III. WOOD FUEL FARMS OR PLANTATIONS

The concept of energy farms or energy plantations[tm],
has captivated the imagination of numerous policy-oriented plan-
ners who, for various reasons, have considered these preserves
as approaches to supplying fuels for society. Thus, the estab-
lishment of such fuel supply systems appears in the National
Energy Plan [25], the Energy Research and Development Administration (ERDA) Plan [26] (now part of the Department of Energy), and
elsewhere. The idea has existed for several years,[8] and again
has caught the fancy of the American public.

The concept of energy farms is a long range one. It is
applicable more to energy supply in the twenty-first century
than the remaining years of this century. It is evaluated here,
however, from a shorter time period perspective to be consistent
with the analytical framework of this text. This discussion is
an attempt to put such time frame considerations in perspective.

A. *Minimum Operating Conditions*

Certain operating assumptions must be made in establishing
the conceptual design of an energy farm. These are found in
papers by Henry [28], Bungay and Ward [18], and Alich and Inman
[29]. These assumptions include land availability, crop

---

[8]*The Chlorella experiment by the Carnegie Institution and
the Arthur D. Little Co., conducted in the 1950s, is but one of
many examples of such proposals [27]. In the Chlorella experiment, harvesting of specially grown aquatic biomass was proposed.
The chlorella would then be turned into fuels. Although the discussion here is on terrestrial energy farms, the earlier experiment is cited to show the existence of the idea previously.*

productivity, and fuel product. Summarizing these assumptions, one finds the following:

(1) a minimum size of 28,500 acres [28];

(2) production of 7-10 tons of dry matter per acre per year [28];

(3) intensive land management of crops, including extensive use of fertilizers [28,18];

(4) the production of liquid fuels and chemical feedstocks [18], electricity, or substitute natural gas (SNG) [29] from the biomass grown and harvested.

Bungay and Ward posit a simplified schematic of such a capital- and energy-intensive system, a schematic reproduced here as Fig. 3.

B. *The Energy Farm Assessment*

Based upon those assumptions, one can ask two questions: (1) is wood the optimum crop for an energy preserve, and (2) can the wood-based energy farm compete, economically, from a net energy delivered or trajectory point of view.

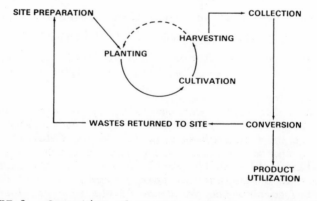

FIGURE 3. Operation of an energy farm. Source: [18].

Numerous authors have addressed the question of how wood stacks up compared to other crop materials. Table VIII provides a comparative assessment in terms of dry tons/acre grown, and energy production potential. It demonstrates clearly that, while some wood species exceed the 10 tons/acre minimum, crops such as sugar cane and sugar beets exhibit superior biomass

TABLE VIII

Annual Productivity and Fuel Production Potential of Selected Biomass Crops

Crop	Annual productivity [18] (tons/acre)[a]	Fuel production potential (10^6 Btu/acre, O.D. basis)
Wood crops		
Loblolly pine	10	160
Aspen	4	60
Poplar	20	320
Eucalyptus	26	420
Agricultural crops		
Corn	16–26	∿280[b]
Wheat	18–30	∿300[b]
Potatoes	22	260
Rye grass	23	280
Sugar cane	64	770
Sugar beets	31–42	450

[a]Assumes midpoint or range.

[b]This tons/acre figure is total biomass production rather than merchantable wood production. Hence it appears larger than the Site Class data. The difference is accounted for by the inclusion of branches, foliage, and other elements of the complete tree.

production rates. Such productivity and yield rates suggest that, if an energy preserve is to be established, it will probably be an energy farm based upon sugar crops, particularly sugar cane. This preferential position of sugar cane and sugarbeets is extended if liquid, alcohol-type fuels are produced in response to society's demands. The sugar crops can yield ∿265 gal/acre of alcohol, compared to ∿180 gal/acre for potatoes, ∿90 gal/acre for corn, and ∿70 gal/acre for wood [27].

Because wood is marginally competitive for some species and above the minimum yield requirement, it is essential to determine if the energy preserve is a useful means for producing liquid fuels, electricity, or SNG. Again trajectory analysis is used in order to stabilize energy economics. Energy efficiency is used as a proxy for economic efficiency.

The trajectory for the energy preserve includes the following steps: growth, extraction, conversion, transport, and combustion. This can be compared to the normal wood trajectory: extraction, transport, and direct combustion. It can also be compared to the trajectory for producing synthetic fuels from coal or oil shale. In a comparison with coal conversion, the final combustion need not be calculated for either fuel.

Table IX details the energy trajectory for wood from the energy preserve to the customer through all stages of activity, showing a net energy production of 20.33%. It assumes intensive forest management practices, whole tree chipping, and conversion to synthetic crude oil although conversion to methanol yields the same result. The trajectory for electricity production gives a value of 24.5%. Figure 4 graphically depicts the liquefaction trajectory and shows that losses go far beyond the acceptable level. Although neither Table IX nor Fig. 4 shows net values for normal wood fuel use as described in Chapter 4, or coal liquefaction, those trajectories have been calculated.

TABLE IX

Detailed Energy Trajectory of the Wood-Based Energy Farm
Producing Liquid Fuels (in 10^{12} Btu)

Total energy to be grown	1000
Wood-growing energy costs [30]	
Cultivation and planting	0.5
Fertilization	32.5
Subtotal	33.0
Extraction energy costs [30]	
Felling and bunching	4.4
Skidding	6.2
Chipping	4.7
Transport to stockpile	6.2
Auxiliary	3.7
Subtotal	25.2
Conversion energy costs[a]	667.0
Transportation energy costs[b]	21.5
Final combustion energy costs[c]	50.0
Net energy delivered	203.3
Trajectory efficiency	20.33%

[a] Assumes hydrogenation or described in Chapter 4.

[b] Assumes putting liquid fuel in national energy transportation system; therefore, uses 2.15% energy budget.

[c] Losses are taken only from liquid fuel produced.

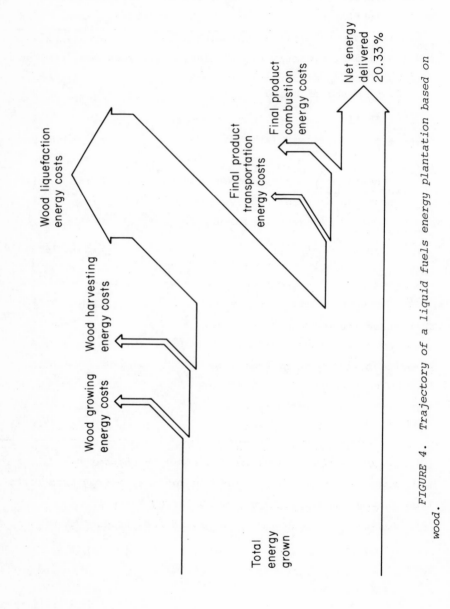

FIGURE 4. Trajectory of a liquid fuels energy plantation based on wood.

The net efficiencies are 65.3 and 52.8%, respectively.[9] From
these data two conclusions can be drawn: (1) it is more economically efficient to use wood in the traditional manner than to
establish an energy plantation with a 20.3% trajectory efficiency;
and (2) if SNG, electricity, or liquids are required, coal and
oil shale are more energetically efficient pathways for their
production. The recent resurgence of oil shale [24], which could
be contributing some 2×10^{15} Btu to the economy by the end of
the century, is particularly damaging to the energy preserve or
farm.

Another comparison can be made between the relative utility
of biomass and coal for supplying liquefaction systems: the
amount of land required to deliver 1×10^{12} Btu of feedstock to
a conversion facility. For forest fuel systems delivering wood
with a 35% moisture content, the land requirement is 9600 acres
disturbed per year. For coal production in western surface
mines, assuming 10 ft thick seams and 80% extraction efficiency,
only 3.5 acres need to be disturbed each year [31]. For
Illinois coal, assuming a 5 ft thick seam mined by underground
room-and-pillar systems operating at 50% extraction efficiency,
11.1 acres need to be utilized each year. If one projects this
line of reasoning further, comparing the amount of land required
to deliver 10^{12} Btu to the economy in the form of liquid fuels
or SNG, the disparity becomes so enormous that it approaches the
absurd.

There are other criticisms of energy farming outside the
productivity, trajectory, and land arguments. Grantham argues
that the costs of land, water, and fertilizer required by an
energy preserve will preclude using forests specifically for
energy purposes [32]. Fiber production generates a greater
return on investment. Eimers [33] points out that forest fuel

---

[9]*It is generally acknowledged that oil shale is still more
efficient than coal for the production of liquids.*

preserves will not attract investment capital. He demonstrates
that on tree crops with more than a four-year rotation, the
return on investment is less than 5%, a rate that is totally
inadequate for attracting risk capital. In short, energy crops
of wood (and probably of other plants as well) cannot be considered as potentially available in this century or for some time
beyond.

IV. CONCLUSIONS

For the remainder of this century then, wood fuels will come
from the residues of forest management, forest harvesting, and
forest products manufacturing. Such fuels, plus wood harvested
for residential consumption, can be produced economically at a
rate commensurate with nuclear power. During this period wood
from energy plantations will not make a measurable contribution.

Wood fuel reserves of the twenty-first century, while beyond
the scope of this text, may include some material harvested from
energy plantations. This will be most probable if E. S.
Lipinsky's "adaptive systems" are adopted [34]. Adaptive systems
are flexible production units designed to produce fiber and
energy for sale. They are basically an extension of current
pulp and paper practice. For the foreseeable future, however,
these remain speculative resources rather than wood fuel reserves
if the analogy is redrawn.

The ultimate question is neither resources nor reserves.
Rather it is projected consumption of wood fuels. It is projected consumption which ultimately defines the role and position of wood fuels among the total family of fuels for the U.S.
economy.

REFERENCES

1. Committee on Renewable Resources for Industrial Materials (CORRIM), Biological Productivity of Renewable Resources Used as Industrial Materials. Washington, D.C.: National Research Council, National Academy of Sciences, 1976.

2. John I. Zerbe, Conversion of stagnated timber stands to productive sites and use of noncommercial material for fuel, in Fuels and Energy From Renewable Resources (David A. Tillman, Kyosti V. Sarkanen, and Larry L. Anderson, eds.). New York: Academic Press, 1977.

3. John A. Alich Jr. et al., An Evaluation of the Use of Agricultural Residues as an Energy Feedstock – a Ten Site Survey, Vol. II. Menlo Park, California: Stanford Research Institute, July, 1977.

4. The CORRIM Committee, Renewable Resources for Industrial Materials. Washington, D.C.: The National Research Council, National Academy of Sciences, 1976.

5. U.S. Forest Service, The Outlook for Timber in the United States. Washington, D.C.: USGPO, Oct., 1973.

6. H. V. Vaux, Timber resource prospects, in Timber! (William A. Duerr, ed.). Ames, Iowa: Iowa State Univ. Press 1973.

7. National Materials Advisory Board, Problems and Legislative Opportunities in the Basic Materials Industries. Washington, D.C.: National Academy of Sciences, 1975.

8. U.S. Forest Service, The Feasibility of Utilizing Forest Residues for Energy and Chemicals. Washington, D.C.: National Science Foundation, March, 1976.

9. Egon Glesinger, The Coming Age of Wood. New York: Simon & Schuster, 1949.

10. Personal communication from Dr. Earl T. Hayes, Retired Deputy Director, U.S. Bur. of Mines, Dec. 29, 1977.

11. Earl T. Hayes, Energy implications of materials processing, Science 191, Feb. 20, 1976.

12. John B. Grantham, Status of Timber Utilization on the Pacific Coast. Portland, Oregon: U.S. Dept. of Agriculture, Forest Service, 1974.

13. Ingemar Falkehag, Utility of organic renewable resources, *in* Engineering Implications of Chronic Materials Scarcity (James L. Holt, ed.). Washington, D.C.: Congress of the United States, Office of Technology Assessment, April, 1977.

14. Full tree utilization. Jaakko Poyry and Co., 1977.

15. D. W. Goheen, Low molecular weight chemicals, *in* Lignins: Occurrence, Formation, Structure and Reactions (K. V. Sarkanen and C. H. Ludwig, eds.). New York: Wiley (Interscience), 1971.

16. C. H. Hoyt and D. W. Goheen, Polymeric products, *in* Lignins: Occurrence, Formation, Structure and Reactions, (K. V. Sarkanen and C. H. Ludwig, eds.). New York: Wiley (Interscience), 1971.

17. Franklin W. Herrick and Herbert L. Hergert, Utilization of chemicals from wood: Retrospect and Prospect, *in* The Recent Advances in Phytochemistry, Vol. II: The Structure Biosynthesis, and Degradation of Wood (Frank A. Loewus and V. C. Runeckles, eds.). New York: Plenum, 1977.

18. Henry R. Bungay and Roscoe F. Ward, Fuels and chemicals from crops, *in* Fuels From Waste (Larry L. Anderson and David A. Tillman, eds.). New York: Academic Press, 1977.

19. D. W. Goheen and J. T. Henderson, The preparation of unsaturated hydrocarbons from lignocellulosic materials. Presented at the International Wood Chemistry Symposium, Seattle, Washington, Sept. 1-4, 1969.

20. D. W. Goheen, J. V. Orle, and R. P. Wither, Indirect pyrolysis of Kraft black liquors, *in* Thermal Uses and Properties of Carbohydrates and Lignins (Fred Shafizadeh, Kyosti V. Sarkanen, and David A. Tillman, eds.). New York: Academic Press, 1976.

21. Ronald S. Wishart, Industrial energy in transition: A petrochemical perspective, Science 199, No. 4329, Feb. 10, 1978.

22. Energy Materials Resources Group, Executive Summary (background paper). Prepared for the Committee on Nuclear and Alternative Energy Systems, Nat. Acad. of Sci., Jan. 1977.

23. James Boyd and L. T. Silver, United States uranium position. Prepared for the ASME-IEEE Joint Power Conference, Long Beach, California, Sept. 18-21, 1977.

24. Thomas H. Maugh II, Oil shale prospects on the upswing... Again, Science 198, No. 4321, Dec. 9, 1977.

25. The Executive Office of the President, The National Energy Plan. Washington, D.C.: USGPO, 1977.

26. A National Plan for Energy Research, Development and Demonstration: Creating Choices for the Future, Vol. I. Washington, D.C.: U.S. Energy Research and Development Administration, 1976.

27. Hans Thirring, Energy for Man. New York: Harper and Row, 1976.

28. J. F. Henry, M. D. Frazer, and C. W. Vail, The energy plantation: Design operation and economic potential, *in* Thermal Uses and Properties of Carbohydrates and Lignins (Fred Shafizadeh, Kyosti V. Sarkanen, and David A. Tillman, eds.). New York: Academic Press, 1976.

29. J. A. Alich Jr., and R. E. Inman, Utilization of plant biomgas as an energy feedstock, *in* Energy, Agriculture and Waste Management (William J. Jewell, ed.). Ann Arbor, Michigan: Ann Arbor Science Publ., 1975.

30. N. Smith and T. J. Corcoran, The energy analysis of wood
     production for fuel applications, *in* Preprints of Papers
     Presented at New York, New York, April 5–9, 1976, 21, No. 2.
     Washington, D.C.: American Chemical Society, 1976.

31. Environmental Studies Board, National Academy of Sciences,
     Rehabilitation Potential of Western Coal Lands. Cambridge,
     Massachusetts: Ballinger, 1974.

32. John B. Grantham, Anticipated competition for available
     wood fuels in the United States, *in* Fuels and Energy From
     Renewable Resources (David A. Tillman, Kyosti V. Sarkanen,
     and Larry L. Anderson, eds.). New York: Academic Press,
     1977.

33. Kirk L. Eimers, Short rotation forestry: A renewable energy
     supply. Presented before the American Institute of Chemi-
     cal Engineers, Nov. 28–Dec. 2, 1976.

34. John B. Grantham *et al.*, Energy and Raw Material Potentials
     of Wood Residue in the Pacific Coast States. Portland,
     Oregon: U.S. Dept. of Agriculture, Forest Service, 1974.

35. E. S. Lipinsky, Fuels from biomass: Integration with food
     and materials systems, Science 199, No. 4329, Feb. 10, 1978.

36. J. A. Knight *et al.*, Pyrolytic conversion of agricultural
     wastes to fuels. Presented before the Annual Meeting of
     the American Society of Agricultural Engineers, Stillwater,
     Oklahoma, June, 1974.

Chapter 8

THE FUTURE USE
OF WOOD FUELS

I. INTRODUCTION

The assessment of wood fuels in the preceding chapters developed certain perspectives essential to projecting the future use of this energy resource. Before launching into projections of wood fuels consumption to the year 2000, it is essential to review and summarize these historical, technical, and resource perspectives. From such an analytical base, consumption can be forecast. From such forecasts the future role and position of wood fuels, within the total family of fuels can be ascertained.

It should be noted, at the outset, that all energy forecasts rely upon some price assumptions. As has been observed in Chapter 7, Hayes estimates an average cost of energy in 1985 of $4/10^6$ Btu. The recently completed Tenneco-Algeria agreement on natural gas sets a price on that fuel at $4.50/10^6$ Btu. That Algerian contract effectively establishes the current marginal price of energy and it substantiates the position taken by Hayes. Thus, this author assumes at least the $4/10^6$ Btu economy in 1985. It is in that light that the previous perspectives reviewed below and the subsequent projection of energy supply should be considered.

A.   *A Summary of Wood Fuel Perspectives*

Wood, once the primary fuel of the U.S. economy, lost its
dominant position due to industrialization. Although consumption of wood fuels declined for a time, it has rebounded
recently. Now wood is a strong supplementary, special-purpose
fuel. While it is used in residential applications, its strength
comes from utilization in forest industries and wood-producing
regions. Synergistic forces of energy price and environmental
protection cost have made it increasingly attractive. Today
some 1.6×10^{15} Btu of energy are supplied to the U.S. economy
by wood, a quantity that is growing substantially as wood fuel
markets expand. While the basic support for wood as a fuel
comes from pulp and paper mills, sawmills, and plywood and veneer
operations, that base of support is broadening.

Wood fuels have a broad range of energy contents which, for
the most part, are somewhat lower in value than the fossil fuels
but higher in value than the other vegetation or waste-based
fuels. Because the energy content of all wood fuels is less concentrated than the fossil fuels, their transportation radius is
limited to about 30 miles in traditional situations, and about
100-200 miles in optimal situations. This varying energy content
of wood fuels vis-a-vis fossil fuels also means that energy
recovery by combustion or conversion can be somewhat less efficient than that for coal. Such efficiency ranges from ∿60-80%.
These inefficiences constrain but do not eliminate competition
between wood fuels and other fuels. Further, such relative disadvantages can be compensated for and overcome by advanced
systems like co-generation. Wood fuels are in a most advantageous situation with respect to co-generation, for that utilization system is particularly appropriate in the pulp and paper
industry and in integrated forest products complexes. In the
above described context, many wood fuels are eminently useful.

Finally, from a resource point of view, the forest resource base, if managed more intensively, will permit an expansion of wood fuel utilization. Wood fuel consumption could help support increased management activities designed to improve the productivity of the forest resource base through residue utilization; thus a potential new synergy exists, again promoting the use of wood fuels.

In summary, wood is a growing supplementary fuel source which, although limited to regional markets, can capitalize upon certain market-oriented and technical features plus an increasingly productive resource base. Wood fuels can play a larger role in energy supply to the U.S. economy over the remaining years of this century. Will they do so?

B. The Technique for Projecting the Future Role and Position of Wood

In order to define the future role and position of wood, three tasks must be performed: (1) establish an estimated total U.S. energy budget or requirement to the year 2000, (2) project the total use of wood fuels to the year 2000, and compare that contribution to total U.S. energy consumption, and (3) consider the use of other fuels (e.g., nuclear power) in the remainder of this century, compare wood to those fuels, and establish relationships based upon such comparisons. Critical to this assessment are the following assumptions: (1) energy demand is determined by economic activity, (2) wood fuels demand is also determined by economic activity within specific consuming sectors, and (3) consumption of any given fuel is determined by its quality and its resource availability.

II.   THE DEMAND FOR ENERGY IN THE U.S.

Energy consumption to the year 2000 has been the subject of much study, speculation, and writing. Those individuals intimately associated with such projections often disagree on what variables to use, the relative importance of certain variables, and the techniques for generating the projections themselves. Thus it is not surprising that energy requirement forecasts vary by as much as 300%. Amory B. Lovins, in Soft Energy Paths, supports the thesis that energy demand will rise slowly to the turn of the century and then decline in absolute terms to about 75×10^{15} Btu [1]. The U.S. Bureau of Mines forecasts growth to 163.4×10^{15} Btu in the year 2000 by using linear extrapolation techniques based upon gross economic activity measures [2]. Both projections briefly described above are somewhat open ended, based upon the "what we would like to see" assumptions. They are all predicated upon either fundamentally changing life styles or rigidly maintaining present economic relationships.

Perhaps the best estimates developed to date are those of Charles M. Mottley [3], whose studies documented civilian employment as the independent variable that drives energy consumption.[1] Consequently, as Fig. 1 shows, Mottley based future energy demand forecasts upon population and employment projections. Further, he factored various levels of energy conservation into these forecasts. Such rates were 1.56×10^9 Btu/ civilian employee/year at 0% conservation, 1.48×10^9 Btu/ civilian employee/year at 25% conservation, and 1.40×10^9 Btu/ civilian employee/year at 50% conservation in the year 2000 [3]. The resulting forecasts are depicted in Fig. 2.

[1] Multiple-regression models demonstrated that civilian employment was so dominant that it all but obliterated the influence of total population, Gross National Product, and other traditional energy projection parameters.

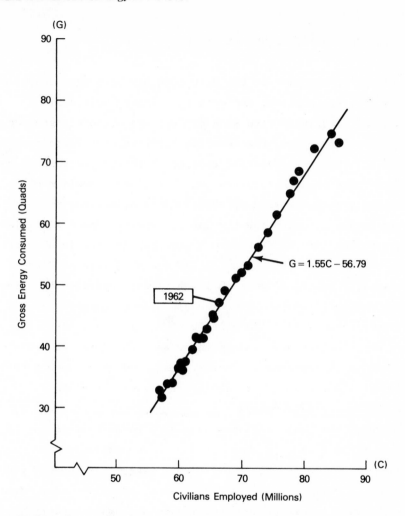

*FIGURE 1. Relation of gross energy to civilian employment,
developed by C. Mottley [3].*

These energy consumption forecasts appear well within the
realm of possibility--both from a supply and utilization stand-
point. They involve neither excessive changes in life style nor
artificial stimulation of the energy sector of the economy. For
that reason they are employed here. Specifically the 25% conservation level is considered as the reference forecast,
recognizing that technologies such as co-generation make that
level of conservation economically available and prudent. For

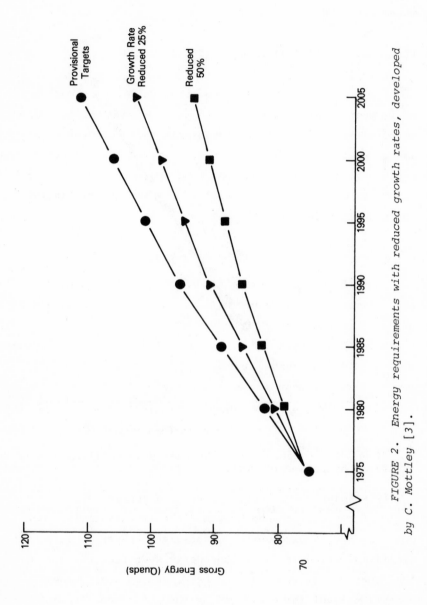

FIGURE 2. Energy requirements with reduced growth rates, developed by C. Mottley [3].

purposes of this discussion, energy consumption in the year 1985 is estimated at 85×10^{15} Btu, and in the year 2000 it is estimated to be 98×10^{15} Btu.[2]

III. THE USE OF WOOD FUELS TO THE YEAR 2000

The economic factor driving total energy consumption is employment. This contrasts with the economic variable driving wood fuels consumption; that variable is manufacturing output among the forest products industries. To a lesser extent manufacturing output of downstream wood products industries such as furniture mills and residential wood fuels consumption will influence the use of this fuel source.

A. *Product Output in the Forest Products Industries*

The U.S. Forest Service has forecast future demand for lumber, plywood, building board (e.g., particle board), and paper products to the year 2000 under varying assumptions [4]. Using the projections that are consistent with the harvest forecasts presented in Chapters 6 and 7, one can predict substantial growth in the forest products industries led by the building board and pulp and paper industries. Table I presents the projected demand for forest products, and the concomitant annual demand growth rates.

The fabrication of downstream products such as furniture and shipping pallets is also expected to increase substantially. The U.S. Forest Service estimates show wood consumption by these industries increasing by 185% between now and the year

[2]*These estimates should be no particular cause of comfort or complacency. The 98 quad requirement represents a 30% growth in energy demand over present levels. It must be met while domestic oil and natural gas production continue to decline. The nonoil and nongas industries must grow at 4.75% annually if oil imports are to be held constant.*

TABLE I

Projected Demand for Products of the Forest Products Industries [4][a]

| Product | Units | Year | | | Change 1970–2000 (%) | Annual growth rate 1970–2000 (%) |
		1970	1985	2000		
Lumber	10^9 bd ft	34.7	35.8	41.5	19.6	0.6
Plywood	10^9 ft^2 3/4 in. basis	15.9	21.1	27.0	69.8	1.7
Building board[b]	10^9 ft^2 3/8 in. basis	9.2	17.8	26.4	186.9	3.6
Pulp and paper	10^6 tons	58.1	97.6	153.5	164.2	3.3

[a]U.S. Forest Service mid case estimates. These projections are virtually the only ones available. Because they were made before the 1973 oil embargo, they may need to be revised downward in light of changing economics. This is particularly true for pulp and paper.

[b]Includes particleboard, insulation board, etc.

2000 [4]. More families will be formed, homes built and furn-
ished, heavy products shipped, and wood consumed as society
progresses.

There are other valid reasons behind such an increase in
wood utilization. Wood products manufacturing requires significantly less energy than the production of its competitors:
aluminum, steel, cement, plastics, etc. Further, the manufacture of wood products generates less unusable residue than the
production of mineral-based competitors [5].

B. Estimates of Wood Fuel Use

From these output projections, one can forecast wood fuel
utilization patterns based upon the total energy required per
unit of output. Table II presents an enumeration of those
energy requirement estimates as of 1972, the base year employed
by the Federal Government for conservation level estimation. It
then presents such factors, employing a 12.5% conservation rate
for 1985 and a 25% rate for the year 2000.

TABLE II

Energy Consumed per Unit of Product Output to the Year 2000

Industry	Unit	1972 [6] Consumption	1985 Consumption[a]	2000 Consumption[b]
Lumber	Btu/bd ft	3.1×10^3	2.7×10^3	2.3×10^3
Plywood[c]	Btu/ft^2	4.4×10^3	3.9×10^3	3.3×10^3
Paper	Btu/ton	33.0×10^6	28.9×10^6	25.0×10^6

[a]Assumes a 12.5% reduction from 1972.

[b]Assumes a 25% reduction from 1972.

[c]This estimate is also used for particleboard and related
products.

A related estimate is then presented showing the degree to
which wood-based energy will be used in wood product manufacture.
It has been shown in Chapter 2 that wood fuels are being employed
increasingly in the forest products industries. Similarly it was
shown in Chapter 5 that these industries can gain significantly
by applying co-generation systems to their own fuels. It is
recognized that cheap hydroelectric power in the Pacific Northwest places economic limits on such drives for energy self-
sufficiency. Because of such limits, total fuel independence
can not be postulated.[3] Table III summarizes the posited rates
of energy self-sufficiency in the wood products industry for
1972, 1985, and the year 2000.

TABLE III

Present and Projected Degree of Energy Self-Sufficiency in the
Forest Products Industries

Industry	Degree of energy self-sufficiency (%) [6,8]			
	1972	1976	1985	2000
Lumber	30	30	45	60[a]
Plywood	50	50	65	80
Pulp and Paper	40	45	62	80

[a]This estimate is lower than the plywood and paper industries
due to the concentration of activity on the west coast where
cheap hydroelectric power exists.

[3]Near energy self-sufficiency, on an overall basis, is possible in large part as a result of the 0.75 quads of salable power
available to the rest of the economy from co-generation facilities in the forest products industries, as estimated by
Johanson and Sarkanen [7].

Tables II and III show the convergence of two forces: declining total energy consumption per unit of product manufactured and increasing reliance on wood based fuels. From these estimates plus projected forest products manufacture, projected consumption of wood fuels by the forest products industries is derived.

The technique employed for obtaining these aggregate estimates involved multiplying the energy required per unit of product by the total projected manufacturing output for each forest industry. These values were then multiplied by the fractions (or percentage/100) of energy to be supplied by wood, values equal to the level of energy independence presented in Table III. Estimates were made for each forest industry for the years 1985 and 2000. These estimates were then summed. TABLE IV is a summary of these projections showing growth in the forest industries' consumption of wood fuels rising from the present level of 1.1 to 3.3×10^{15} Btu in the year 2000.

Previously, projections of wood fuels by downstream and non-wood industries were made by considering the relationships between the forest industries and the downstream firms to be constant [9]. It was assumed that the forest industries would,

TABLE IV

Wood Fuels Consumption in the Forest Products Industry
(in 1×10^{15} Btu)

	Projected wood fuel consumption	
Industry	*1985*	*2000*
Lumber	*0.05*	*0.06*
Plywood and construction board	*0.10*	*0.14*
Pulp and paper	*1.75*	*3.10*
Total	*1.90*	*3.30*

for the next several years, consume 93% of the wood fuels used
in industry. Others would use 7%.

As was shown in Chapter 2, however, the downstream wood
products companies such as furniture mills and pallet manufacturers, and nonwood operations such as green houses, are increasing their share of the wood fuel market. Such use of wood fuel
is based upon local or regional availability of this energy
source. These industries are increasing their share of the
wood fuel market, and they are growing at a rate consistent with
that being experienced by plywood and paper producers. Thus it
is assumed that downstream and nonwood products companies will
increase their share of the industrial wood fuels market from
the present 7% level to 8% in 1985 and 9% in the year 2000.
Thus wood fuel consumption by such firms will rise from its present rate of 0.11×10^{15} Btu per year to 0.17×10^{15} Btu in
1985 and 0.32×10^{15} Btu in the year 2000.

The most nebulous category to project is residential consumption including charcoal utilization. It has been shown that
spectacular growth occurred during the early 1970s. Furthermore,
people are purchasing wood-burning stoves and even systems that
convert household furnaces from oil to wood [11]. For projection
purposes, however, it has been assumed that wood fuel consumption
in homes would rise from 0.42 to 0.5×10^{15} Btu between 1976
and 1985 and remain at that level through the rest of the
century [9].

The experience in Maine and Vermont helps explain why residential wood fuel consumption would double between 1970 and 1976,
but not rise by much after that. In Maine, it is estimated that
75% of the homes now are equipped to use wood for heating purposes [11]. In Vermont, where 54% of the homes have wood stoves
for heating and 6% have wood-fired central heating systems,
about 40% of the wood fuel utilization systems were installed
between 1974 and 1976 [1]. In those areas, at least, there has

been phenomenal growth recently; and there is far less room for
future growth. Maine and Vermont may be viewed as typical
prime wood fuel using areas.

Total wood fuels consumption in industrial and residential
applications then, will increase from the present level of 1.59
to 4.12×10^{15} Btu by the year 2000, as Table V shows. Over the
next 24 years, wood will increase its contribution to the
economy by 160%, growing at an annual rate of 4.05%. As can be
expected, the forest industries will lead the way.

C. Supply-Consumption Balances

One can question if the wood will be available to supply
4.12×10^{15} Btu to the economy. After all, that represents
nearly 260×10^{6} tons, or 17×10^{9} ft^{3} of biomass. One could
cover 425 thousand acres a foot deep with that much wood.

TABLE V

Projected Wood Fuel Utilization to the Year 2000 (in 10^{15} Btu)[a]

	1976[a]	1985	2000	Annual growth rate (%) 1976–2000
Forest industries	1.05	1.90	3.30	4.89
Other industries	0.12	0.17	0.32	4.17
Residential	0.42	0.50	0.50	0.73
Total	1.59	2.57	4.12	4.05

[a]Actual.

[b]These are conservative estimates when compared to other
wood fuels projections, despite the 160% total increase in wood
fuels consumption. For reasons explained in Chapter 7, they
include no electricity from wood save co-generation. They
include no contribution from energy plantations. They include
a very modest amount of wood fuel consumed by nonwood industries
and treat residential wood fuel use almost as a constant.

However, 4.12×10^{15} Btu can be produced from the residues of forestry, wood harvesting, and forest products manufacture. Figure 3 shows the relationship between projected wood fuel producibility and projected wood fuel consumption.

As Fig. 3 shows, there is presently a surplus of potential fuel wood generated annually equal to 1.65×10^{15} Btu. This will decline to 1.5×10^{15} Btu in 1985 and 0.4×10^{15} Btu in the year 2000. If one assumes that 4% of the unmarketable timber is made available annually, then the current surplus is 2.7×10^{15} Btu. The 1985 surplus will be 2.1×10^{15} Btu.

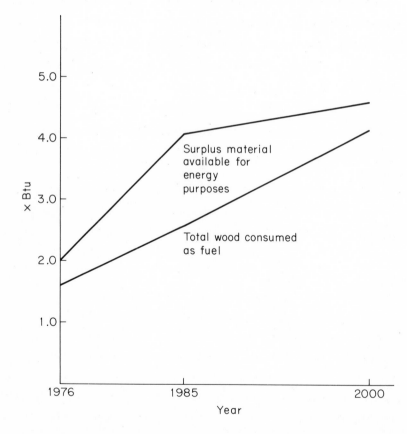

FIGURE 3. The projected availability and fuel utilization of wood residues.

A surplus of 1.1×10^{15} Btu will be available in the year 2000.
If one assumes portions of the total biomass not included in
these estimates (e.g., branches and foliage), the surplus available will be still significantly larger. Such reserves, plus
growth in the forest industries, will support additional wood
fuel utilization in the twenty-first century.

IV. THE POSITION AND ROLE OF WOOD FUELS

Comparative analysis with other fuels has been the evaluation
technique employed throughout the entire book. Such a comparison
is essential here if the contribution of wood fuels is to be
placed in the context of total energy policies and programs, in
the context of the total family of fuels.

A. *The Position of Forest Fuels*

Forest fuels are among the numerous supplementary fuels
available to the economy; their contribution should be understood
within that context. Such fuels include: (1) urban-industrial
and agricultural wastes, (2) nuclear power, (3) hydroelectric
power, (4) shale oil, (5) geothermal heat, and (6) solar energy.
Independent forecasts have been run for virtually all of the
supplementary fuels. Presented below are the results of such
forecasts.

The recovery of energy from urban-industrial and agricultural
residues is now being practiced regularly. MSW is incinerated
to produce steam as is shown in Fig. 4, co-combusted with coal,
and pyrolyzed into gaseous or liquid fuels. Agricultural
residues are also incinerated to produce steam. Bagasse incineration with heat recovery supplies over 60% of that industry's
energy requirement [12]. Cotton gin waste incineration is also
rapidly growing. Additionally, several anaerobic digestion
plants are expected to come on stream between now and 1980,

FIGURE 4.   The $35 million Wheelabrator-Frye RESCO municipal
waste-to-energy system in Saugus, Massachusetts. (Photo courtesy
of Wheelabrator-Frye Corp.)

producing methane gas from feedlot manure. It is projected that
in 1985, urban wastes will be supplying 0.37×10^{15} Btu and
agricultural materials 0.35×10^{15} Btu; in the year 2000, those
energy sources will be supplying 1.0 and 0.67×10^{15} Btu
respectively, if anticipated growth rates hold [9].

    There is ample evidence to demonstrate that these growth
rates are conservative. The questionnaire survey we ran at
Area Development Magazine in September, 1977, showed that 15%
of the firms responding are planning to use their own wastes as
a source of fuel. These firms represented over 50% of the 211
manufacturing facilities covered by questionnaire responses.
Their products ranged from petrochemicals to aircraft. Of the

firms planning expansions, 29% are planning to use in-plant wastes as one source of fuel. The 29% represents some 67% of the manufacturing facilities covered. Among fuels for expanding industry in-plant waste ranked fourth, right behind oil, electricity, and coal.

Nuclear power, once heralded as the successor to oil, is now considered to be of limited availability. As Chapter 7 showed, its maximum producibility is 2.3×10^{15} Btu in 1985 and 4.8×10^{15} Btu in the year 2000.[4] This assumes no breeder technology at least to the end of this century. Nuclear power, then, will be slightly stronger than wood; it will, however, not match the output of all biomass resources.

The projection for hydroelectric power used is that made by the U.S. Bureau of Mines. It shows growth from the present 3.1 to 6.1×10^{15} Btu in the year 2000 [13]. The forecast for shale oil employed relies upon the renewed optimum expressed by Science [14]. One can reasonably expect 1.0×10^{15} Btu from oil shale by the year 2000.

The forecasts for geothermal and solar energy systems are based upon the Ford Foundation study. The results show that, without significant levels of artificial stimulation, the combined output of these resources probably will not exceed 0.5×10^{15} Btu in the year 2000 [15].

Figure 5 is a pictorial summary of the growth of supplementary fuels between now and the year 2000. It shows growth from the 1976 level of 6.9 to 18.2×10^{15} Btu in the year 2000. This entire forecast is quite similar to that made by Earl T. Hayes [16]. It shows annual growth rates of 3.62% for the period 1976-1985, 4.43% for the period 1985-2000, and 4.12% for the

---

[4] As with hydroelectric power, nuclear numbers show the output as electricity rather than the input as water or uranium. The reason is that these energy systems can only deliver one form of energy.

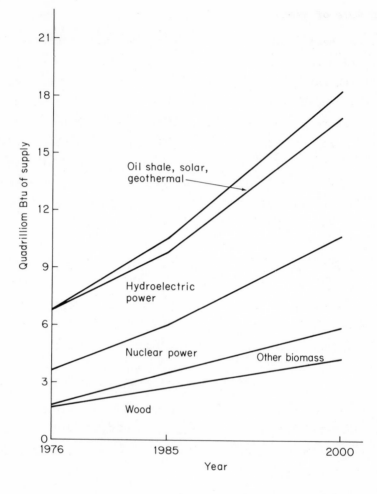

FIGURE 5.   *Projected supply of supplementary fuels in the*
year 2000.

overall period 1976–2000.   In the overall picture, the supplementary fuels will increase their aggregate contribution to
total energy supply from the present level of 8.3% to a projected level of 18.6% in the year 2000.   These fuels will make
contributions in specific economic sectors or geographic regions
where they are most appropriate.

B. *The Role of Wood Fuels*

It has been shown that wood fuels alone will increase their
contribution from 1.6 to 4.1×10^{15} Btu. Today wood supplies
2.1% of the nation's energy needs; in the year 2000 the wood
fuels will supply 4.2% of the nation's energy requirements.
Neither figure is earth-shaking, but the combination of an absolute and a relative increase is significant. More impressive,
perhaps, is the fact that between now and the end of the century
total energy consumption will grow by 23×10^{15} Btu, and wood
fuels will provide 11% of the increase, a substantial amount for
fuels that the Federal government does not even bother with in
its data-gathering and analysis activities. Supplementary fuels,
in total, will supply 51% of that 23×10^{15} Btu energy supply
increase.

In growing from 1.6 to 4.1×10^{15} Btu, wood fuels will
remain within the confines of the forces identified by the historical and value assessments. They will be industry specific
and regionally significant. They will be the dominant fuels in
the forest industries and, to a lesser extent, in other wood-
consuming industries. They will be used broadly in such areas
as northern New England, the northern Midwest (e.g., Michigan,
Wisconsin, Minnesota), and other wood-producing regions that
lack significant supplies of indigenous fossil fuels. Wood will
intensify its position as a supplementary fuel: one whose sudden
disruption will cause serious problems in select industries and
regions, but not seriously cripple the national economy.

In becoming entrenched as a supplementary fuel, wood will
provide an example of the only approach available to this
nation's energy dilemma. This nation must turn away from overdependence on one or a few national fuels and look to a broad
base of industry-specific, region-specific, or application-
specific (e.g., liquid fuels for transportation) energy sources.
Serving as an example of the long-term energy solution is,

perhaps, the most important role that wood fuels can play. Wood
fuels are reasonably attractive to specific industries and
regions. They are not nearly so attractive or available that
society will become as dependent on them as it has become on oil.
Energy supply is somewhat like carpentry: there is a proper tool
for every job, and the well-outfitted carpenter has a wide
diversity of tools, not just a hammer. Wood fuels are among
society's many potential energy tools.

The industrial sector of the U.S. economy is beginning to
take this approach, diversifying its energy supply. The Area
Development questionnaire demonstrated that manufacturing firms
are now turning to not only the traditional oil, electricity,
propane, and coal solutions; but also to wood, in-plant waste,
solar power, and synthetic fuels from coal. They are turning in
droves to waste heat boilers and, where appropriate,
co-generation. They are turning away from natural gas and,
to a lesser extent, petroleum.

C. *The Position and Role of Wood Fuels in Other Nations*

While the role of wood as an energy source will be significant but fairly limited in this country, it will be larger in
developing economies. In Brazil, for example, pulp production
is expected to rise from 1.83 to 35.8 × 10^6 tons by the end of
this century. This expansion will be fueled with wood. Steel
production is expected to become increasingly reliant upon
charcoal. Modest amounts of ethanol for transportation fuel will
also come from wood, with much larger amounts coming from sugar
cane. In order to accomplish this, Brazil will harvest eucalyp-
tus trees on five-year rotations and will establish numerous
biomass energy plantations [17].

The Brazilian program is in response to their need to industrialize and their lack of significant quantities of indigenous
fossil fuels. Thus wood must play a large role there. The

Workshop on Alternative Energy Strategies, while not specifically analyzing noncommercial fuels including biomass, recognized that they will be highly significant in other developing nations [18]. It cited India, where biomass fuels now supply 48% of the nation's energy, a contribution that must be maintained in absolute if not relative terms.

In the developed economies of Europe, less emphasis is being placed on biomass. However, cooperative research through the European Economic Community is examining the application of short rotation forestry for fuels production [19]. In Canada, the use of forest fuels essentially parallels that being experienced in the U.S. [20].

The role of wood fuels, then, is country specific. The limitation on wood fuels in this country vis-a-vis Brazil, for example, stems from the following forces: (1) the degree of industrialization, (2) the availability of other fuels (e.g., coal), and (3) the climate (hence the rotation time of tree crops). Despite, or because of, such limitations wood remains a prime example of this nation's energy future: a solid, supplementary fuel.

Estimating energy supply and consumption beyond the year 2000 involves making a host of value judgments and assumptions that are outside the scope of this book. Certainly we know that coal resources will be ample, and that oil and gas resources will be of diminishing importance. Beyond that, however, we do not know whether breeder reactors will become politically acceptable; whether fusion power will materialize; or whether conservation, now emerging, can make sufficient impacts on energy demand to stabilize the supply-consumption balances. Certainly we cannot know what long-run population and employment trends will be.

In the absence of such knowledge, it is impossible to forecast energy balances with any degree of confidence. Thus this presentation is confined to a 25-year time horizon: a critical period for energy supply.

V.   CONCLUSION

Wood is a growth fuel among the class of energy sources that
is growing most rapidly: the supplementary fuels. It was once
mankind's only fuel and from there fell to nearly total disuse
as more concentrated energy forms were available and needed to
accomplish the tasks of industrialization. It has made its comeback as a specific use fuel based upon a synergy of energy and
environmental costs. It will increase its contribution based
upon that synergy plus another tandem of forces: advanced energy
recovery systems and advanced silvicultural practices required to
improve the forest resource base.

In its resurgence, wood will set an example of the optimum
energy solution. It has often struck me that an energy solution
leaning toward many fuels supplying modest amounts of energy is
inherently more stable and less problematical than a solution
leaning toward a few fuels supplying vast amounts of energy. To
arrive at the many fuel solution, this economy needs to look to
the example of wood and then seek other similar fuels. The
manufacturing sector is now beginning to take this approach.

There are some marvelous stories told by A. Speer, in his
memoirs concerning running the industries of Nazi Germany during
World War II [21]. Speer points out that the Luftwaffe was
almost totally dependent upon the Luena Works, as were all other
sectors of the war effort requiring liquid fuels. When the
Allies finally got around to bombing those synthetic fuels
plants with reasonable regularity, they effectively shut down
liquid fuel consuming sectors of the war machine. Speer states,
in his memoirs, that on the day when the synthetic fuels plants
were bombed, the technological war was lost. He also points out
that Nazi Germany depended upon only a few ball bearing plants,
and these relied upon one basic hydroelectric complex. Had the
allies consistently bombed that complex, the German war machine
could not have continued to operate and the war would have

ended many months sooner than it did. These stories provide stark substantiation of the dangers of the "few fuels" option.

Fortunately this nation's energy alternatives are far more diverse than those that were available to Nazi Germany. It is, therefore, wood's primary role to grow, and to illustrate an energy policy that diversifies energy sources to the point where overdependence on one or another fuel is avoided. Yes, we will use oil and gas, coal and synthetic fuels from coal, shale oil, nuclear power, and the like. But, as the example of wood shows and as the stories of Speer hightlight, there need not and should not be excessive commitment to one or a few fuels, to one or a few supply options. In that context wood is a key fuel for America's future.

REFERENCES

1. Amory B. Lovins, Soft Energy Paths: Toward a Durable Peace. Cambridge, Massachusetts: Ballinger, 1977.

2. Walter G. Dupree Jr. and John S. Corsetino, United States Energy to the Year 2000 (Revised). Washington, D.C.: U.S. Dept. of the Interior, Dec., 1975.

3. Charles M. Mottley, How much energy do we really need, in Fuels and Energy From Renewable Resources (David A. Tillman, Kyosti V. Sarkanen, and Larry L. Anderson, eds.). New York: Academic Press, 1977.

4. U.S. Forest Service, The Outlook for Timber in the United States. Washington, D.C.: USGPO, 1973.

5. Edward P. Cliff, Timber: The Renewable Material. Washington, D.C.: USGPO, Aug., 1973.

6. U.S. Forest Service, The Feasibility of Utilizing Forest Residues for Energy and Chemicals. Washington, D.C.: National Science Foundation, March, 1976.

7. L. N. Johansen and K. V. Sarkanen, Prospects for co-generation of steam and power in the forest products industry, *in* Fuels and Energy From Renewable Resources (David A. Tillman, Kyosti V. Sarkanen, and Larry L. Anderson, eds.). New York: Academic Press, 1977.

8. J. M. Duke and M. J. Fudali, Report on the Pulp and Paper Industry's Energy Savings and Changing Fuel Mix. New York: American Paper Institute, Sept., 1976.

9. David A. Tillman, Combustible renewable resources, Chemtech 7, No. 10, Oct., 1977.

10. Bill White, Convert Your Oil Furnace to Wood. Danielson, Connecticut: William P. White, 1976.

11. David Pauly with Richard Manning, They're cooking with wood, Newsweek, Jan. 2, 1978.

12. William Arlington, Bagasse as a renewable resource, *in* Fuels and Energy From Renewable Resources (David A. Tillman, Kyosti V. Sarkanen, and Larry L. Anderson, eds.). New York: Academic Press, 1977.

13. Walter Dupree, Herman Enzer, Stanley Miller, and David Miller, Energy Perspectives 2. Washington, D.C.: U.S. Dept. of the Interior, June, 1976.

14. Thomas H. Maugh II, Oil shale prospects on the upswing... Again, Science 198, No. 4321, Dec. 9, 1977.

15. Spurgeon M. Keeney, Jr. *et al.,* Nuclear Power Issues and Choices. Cambridge, Massachusetts: Ballinger (for the Ford Foundation), 1977.

16. Private communication from Dr. Earl T. Hayes, Energy Consultant, Dec. 29, 1977.

17. The Editors, Discussion of critical issues, *in* Fuels and Energy From Renewable Resources (David A. Tillman, Kyosti V. Sarkanen, and Larry L. Anderson, eds.). New York: Academic Press, 1977.

18. Carol L. Wilson, Energy: Global Prospects 1985-2000.
    Report of the Workshop on Alternative Energy Strategies.
    New York: McGraw-Hill (for the Massachusetts Institute of
    Technology), 1977.

19. Padraig McAllister, International aspects of biomass conver-
    sion, *in* Capturing the Sun Through Bioconversion, Proceed-
    ings. Washington, D.C.: Council on Solar Biofuels, 1976.

20. G. MacNabb, Energy-Canada, Proc. International Biomass
    Energy Conference. Winnipeg, Canada: The Biomass Energy
    Institute, 1973.

21. Albert Speer, Inside the Third Reich. New York: Macmillan,
    1970.

Appendix

UNITS OF MEASURE

I. INTRODUCTION

The preceding text was written in the English system of
measure. It was so written in order to conform to the units of
measure which remain conventional in this country despite the
internal pecularities of the English system. This appendix is
intended to provide those interested readers with Metric equivalents. Beyond general English–Metric conversion are specific
fuel and wood conversion factors essential to the study of
energy. In fuels, the units available are tons (coal), barrels
and gallons (oil), cubic ft (natural gas), kilowatts (electricity), and more. Wood units of measure include (not exhaustive):
board feet, cubic feet, cords, tons, units, cunits, and square
feet (applied to plywood and like products). Each measure was
developed to meet a specific purpose. Unit equivalents depend
on average estimated values.

The author could not possibly go beyond recognizing this
diversity of measuring systems. Thus, presented below are critical conversion factors used in the text. They are provided as a
means for interpreting the data previously presented.

II.   CONVERSION FACTORS

A.   *English-Metric Conversions*

   (a)   1 pound = 454 grams

   (b)   1 bbl (42 gal) = 159.0 liters

   (c)   1 mile = 1.6 kilometers

   (d)   1 acre = 0.404 hectares

   (e)   1 cubic foot - 0.03 cubic meters

   (f)   1 British Thermal Unit = 251.996 calories

   (g)   1 Btu/lb = 0.555 kcal/kg

   (h)   °F × 5/9 (°F + 40°F) - 40°C = °C

B.   *Fuel Conversions*

   (a)   1 quad = 1 × 10^{15} Btu (quadrillion Btu)

   (b)   1 quad = 40 × 10^6 tons bituminous coal;

                 50 × 10^6 tons sub-bituminous coal; and

                 62.5 × 10^6 tons lignite

   (c)   1 quad = 172.4 × 10^6 barrels of oil

   (d)   1 quad = 1 × 10^{12} ft^3 natural gas

   (e)   1 quad = 62.5 × 10^6 tons wood (O.D. basis)

   (f)   1 quad = 96.2 × 10^6 tons wood (green basis)

   (g)   1 quad = 105 × 10^6 tons municipal waste

   (h)   1 quad = 293 × 10^9 kilowatts delivered

   (i)   1 ton bituminous coal = 25 × 10^6 Btu

   (j)   1 barrel of oil = 5.8 × 10^6 Btu

   (k)   1 ft^3 natural gas = 1000 Btu

   (l)   1 ton wood (O.D. basis) = 16 × 10^6 Btu[*]

   (m)   1 ton wood (green basis) = 10.5 × 10^6 Btu[*]

[*]*This is an average. Values for softwoods and hardwoods are
presented in Chapter III. As has been noted value by age of
wood, type of material (e.g., bark, heartwood, etc.), and other
factors.*

(n)   1 ton municipal waste = 9.5×10^6 Btu[*]

(o)   1 kilowatt (delivered) = 3412 Btu

C.   *Wood Conversions*

(a)   1 cub ft $\doteq$ ∿30.0 lbs[**]

(b)   1 cord $\doteq$ ∿1.25 tons[†]

(c)   1 bd ft $\doteq$ ∿2.5 lbs[††]

[*]*This is an average value also, and equally subject to wide variation.*

[**]*1 ft³ softwood $\doteq$ 27 lb and 1 ft³ hardwood $\doteq$ 32 lb on average.*

[†]*A cord is defined as wood stacked in a 4 ft × 4 ft × 8 ft pile. There is much variation in this unit of measure.*

[††]*This is again an approximation.*

INDEX

influence of railroads, 9–10, 26
  use by railroads, 6–7, 11
  use by iron industry, 5, 7–8, 11, 16
influence of oil embargo, 34, 45–46
markets, 26, 34, 42, 220
present consumption, 34–42, 220
reasons for consumption, 27, 43–51, 220
Wood, heating value
  influence of carbon, 69–72, 72–74, 83
  influence of lignin, 65, 67–69
  influence of moisture, 65, 77–83
Wood products industries, 12–14, 19, 21, 26,
    37, 42, 148–152, 164–167, 220, 225–230,
    see also U.S. forest industry

Wood residues
  competition for, 18–19, 188, 198–203
  economics of use, 26, 27, 126–131, 188,
    193–198, 214–215, 221
  quantities of, 188, 189–193, 203, 205–206,
    232–233
  types of
    forest management residues, 188, 189–
      191, 195, 205
    logging residues, 89, 126, 130, 188, 191–
      192, 195, 196, 204, 205
    manufacturing residues, 90, 126, 188
    mill residues, 19, 89, 126, 130, 188, 192–
      193, 194, 204, 205